PELICAN BOOKS

ISLAM

Alfred Guillaume was the Head of the Department of
the Near and Middle East in the School of Oriental
and African Studies, and Professor of Arabic, in the
University of London, and later Visiting Professor of
Arabic in the University of Princeton, New Jersey. He
took up Arabic after studying Theology and Oriental
Languages at the University of Oxford. In the First
World War he served in France and then in the Arab
Bureau in Cairo. He was ordained when he returned to
England. He was known in the Muhammadan world as
the editor of *The Legacy of Islam*, which has been translated into several languages, and as the editor and
translator of one of the most important Arabic works
on philosophical theology. During the Second World
War the British Council invited him to accept a visiting
professorship at the American University of Beirut
where he greatly enlarged his circle of Muslim friends.
The Arab Academy of Damascus and the Royal
Academy of Baghdad honoured him by electing him
to their number, and the University of Stambul chose
him as their first foreign lecturer on Christian and
Islamic theology. He died in 1965.

ISLAM

BY

ALFRED GUILLAUME

PENGUIN BOOKS

Penguin Books Ltd, Harmondsworth, Middlesex, England
Penguin Books Inc., 7110 Ambassador Road, Baltimore, Maryland 21207, U.S.A.
Penguin Books Australia Ltd, Ringwood, Victoria, Australia

—

First published 1954
Second edition (revised) 1956
Reprinted 1961, 1962, 1964, 1966, 1968, 1969, 1971

—

Copyright © the Estate of Alfred Guillaume, 1954, 1956

—

Made and printed in Great Britain
by Hunt Barnard Printing Ltd, Aylesbury
Set in Monotype Bembo

CONTENTS

1. THE HISTORICAL BACKGROUND   I

2. MUHAMMAD   20

3. THE QURĀN   55

4. THE ISLAMIC EMPIRE   78

5. APOSTOLIC TRADITION   88

6. SECTS   III

7. PHILOSOPHY AND THE GENESIS
   OF THE CREEDS   128

8. MYSTICISM   143

9. ISLAM TODAY   155

THE RELATION OF ISLAM TO
CHRISTIANITY   194

GLOSSARY   201

BOOKS FOR FURTHER READING   203

INDEX   207

CHAPTER ONE

THE HISTORICAL BACKGROUND

By Arabia its people understand the land enclosed on the north by the mountains of Asia Minor, on the south by the Indian Ocean, on the east by the mountains of Persia, and on the west by the Mediterranean and the Red Sea. The name itself is comparatively modern and is first used by classical writers. So far as our knowledge goes the first use of the name Arab is on the inscription of the Assyrian king Shalmaneser III, who in the year 853 B.C. defeated a coalition of small western states in which Ahab, king of Israel, took a prominent part, being supported by a certain 'Jundibu the Arab' who, as all recent writers have noticed, appropriately contributed a thousand camels to the allied contingent. From this time onwards kings and queens of the Arabs are mentioned sporadically in cuneiform tablets. These people inhabited the north of the peninsula. The first known use of the term by the Arabs themselves is on an inscription in the Nabataean script which records the exploits of a certain 'King of all the Arabs'. His rule cannot have been recognized farther south than central Arabia.

It can hardly be supposed that a people firmly rooted in North and South Arabia – the latter the Arabia Felix of the classical writers, – possessing a political and tribal organization and considerable military strength, had not a long history behind them, and we should expect to find some mention of them in ancient historical documents. But no such reference by name is to be found. Where we should expect to find Arabs, e.g. in southern Babylonia (*c.* 2600 B.C.);

in and around Egypt and the middle Euphrates (*c.* 2000); and in Palestine and Syria (*c.* 1400), we find that hordes of tribesmen notorious for brigandage, who were a constant menace to the civilized settlements, are mentioned. These people or peoples were known as Habiru (or 'Apiru) and are almost certainly to be identified with the Arabs. If that be so, then the Hebrews of the Old Testament were Arabs,[1] part of the ancient inhabitants of the Arabian peninsula. No convincing explanation of the name Arab has ever been proposed: but if we adopt this identification the meaning of 'Arab, a metathetical form of 'Abir, is 'nomad'. This identification is supported by the meaning which the plural *a'rāb* = nomads often has in the Qurān and in the inscriptions found in South Arabia which mention bedouin.

With the ancient history of Arabia we are not concerned, though it is worth noting that men of Semitic stock inherited and developed the ancient civilization of the Sumerians on which the empires of Babylon and Assyria were based, and others reached a high level of culture in Phoenicia and South Arabia. The name 'Semitic' has been coined from Shem the son of Noah, the reputed ancestor of most of the inhabitants of Arabia: it is now applied to those who speak, or spoke, a form of the ancient Semitic language of which Arabic is the greatest living representative.

In historical times wave upon wave of Arabs have come up from southern and central Arabia and found their way into the settled lands of the fertile crescent, urged on by poverty and hunger. Settlements and oases can support only a limited number of inhabitants; the pasturage of the steppes can support only a limited number of camels and herds, and

1. For the genealogical, historical, and philological reasons for this statement, see my article in *PEQ*, October 1946, pp. 64–85.

when that number is exceeded a war of conquest or annual raids on the settlements are the only alternatives to starvation. Apart from systematic raids on a large scale, almost every year groups of men from the desert came in and gradually settled down on the cultivated land to replace the victims of disease and epidemics. Thus men in the settlements often have relatives among the tribes of the desert, and though there is hostility because of economic distress, there is also a sense of kinship subsisting between them. As we shall see, this state of affairs had a profound influence on the rapid advance of the Muslims in the first century of the hijra,[1] and has determined the course of history to the present day.

The agelong caravan routes which traverse Arabia in all directions indicate that commerce was an important link between the desert and the sown land. In southern Arabia there was a highly developed civilization, Sabaean, Minaean, and Qatabānian, based on agriculture and the spice traffic; and trade with the outside world brought wealth and prosperity to its people more than a thousand years before the Christian era. The Arab kingdoms in the south dammed the watercourses, built castles and temples, and developed the agriculture of their country to a remarkable degree. They pushed their trade centres far into the north. The language of the southerners differed greatly from the Arabic of the northerners, which was to become classical Arabic, and they used a different script. The 'travelling company of Ishmaelites bearing spicery, balm, and myrrh going to carry it down to Egypt'[2] were engaged in this trade, and it is worth noticing that elsewhere[3] they are called Midianite merchantmen.

At Petra until the second century A.D. there was a flourishing trade centre which controlled the caravan route from

1. See p. 19.   2. Genesis 37:25.   3. Verse 28.

South Arabia until the Nabataean kingdom was taken over by the Romans and became part of the Provincia Arabia in A.D. 105. These people occupied a large trading post at al-Hijr, south of Taymā'. Their imposing sepulchral houses can still be seen there. They are mentioned in the Qurān (7:74) where it is said they are dwelling-houses. Still farther north of Palmyra a powerful Arab state was founded and made famous by the beautiful and tragic queen Zenobia (Zaynab), whose memory still survives in Arab legend.

From this brief sketch of the Arabs it will be seen that trading as much as raiding formed the basis of their social and economic life. The former naturally was primarily the affair of the settled Arabs, though the nomads were equally concerned because the caravans had to pass through their territory and they shared indirectly in the profits that resulted by exacting payment for safe conduct through their lands. As we shall see, trading was the Prophet Muhammad's first occupation, and the end of his life was occupied with raids, to which latter a work by one of his earliest biographers is devoted.

In making a survey of the society into which Muhammad was born we cannot ignore the civilizations of Rome, Persia, and Arabia Felix as though the Arabs of what is now known as the Hijāz[1] – the district in which Mecca and Medina are situated – knew nothing about them. True, the bedouin of the interior were for the most part content to live their lives without regard to what was going on around them, but it must not be supposed that they were isolated. Until modern times news could travel only by word of mouth, or more rarely by letter, and it was the caravans which plied across Arabia in all directions to Syria, Egypt, and the Persian

1. In the time of Muhammad it did not run so far south as it does today.

4

border which brought back news of the outside world and also made the Arabs aware of the civilizations around them. Probably news was disseminated as rapidly as it was within the Byzantine empire itself. Those who could read and write were a small minority, but we have no reason to believe that the Arabs of the seventh century were unable to write their names, and indeed there is early evidence to the contrary. But there is no trustworthy record of any Arabic literature before the Qurān. The tribal bards were the repositories of history in the form of verse, which was repeated from generation to generation by professional remembrancers whose memories, by our standards, were often prodigious. Thus, for the study of the background of the society in which Muhammad lived we must rely on the Qurān itself, on what we know from classical writers, on what can be gleaned from pre-Islamic poetry that was written down centuries later, and on what early Muslim authors tell us about their heathen forefathers.

Mecca, like Petra and Palmyra before it, had become important and prosperous through its position in the centre of a trade route. Its merchants had commercial relations with both Persians and Byzantines and sent caravans twice yearly to the north and south. They also had dealings with Abyssinia on the other side of the Red Sea. The Quraysh, the tribe to which Muhammad belonged, formed companies which shared in the profits of these ventures, and the prophet himself travelled to Syria with a caravan carrying the wares dispatched by Khadīja who afterwards became his wife. The town itself was governed by a committee of prominent merchants called the *mala*'.

The Qurān refers to, and is concerned with, three religious groups: heathens, Jews, and Christians. Muhammad's kinsmen and predecessors were heathens; his neighbours numbered many Jews; Christians were known to him from personal intercourse. In Mecca itself there was apparently no organized Christian community, though, as we shall see, there were large settlements of Christians with their own bishops, churches, and monasteries within easy reach of Mecca; indeed it would have been impossible to travel north, south, or east from Mecca without meeting with them. Something must now be said about these three groups.

I. PAGANS

The customs of heathenism have left an indelible mark on Islam, notably in the rites of the pilgrimage (on which more will be said later), so that for this reason alone something ought to be said about the chief characteristics of Arabian paganism. It would seem that in general the ordinary Arab sat somewhat lightly to his religious duties. Sacrifices, which were for the most part communal feasts, were popular, and certain prophylactic rites were fairly widely observed, but at heart the Arab cared little for these things. He was, as he still is, fundamentally an individualist, and if a heathen god did not, or could not, help him to get what he wanted in life, so much the worse for the god. Nevertheless, a certain prestige attached to towns and oases which were centres of pilgrimage and religious ceremonies and, what was more important to the inhabitants, a good deal of profit accrued to the settlements thereby. This was especially true of Mecca with its annual pilgrimage to which the various tribes flocked in the holy month, to the no small gain of the custodians of the holy place.

It would be tedious to the reader to hear about the many

minor gods in the Arabian pantheon, and therefore it seems best to confine ourselves to those mentioned in the Qurān.

The oldest name for God used in the Semitic word consists of but two letters, the consonant 'l' preceded by a smooth breathing, which was pronounced 'Il' in ancient Babylonia, 'El' in ancient Israel. The relation of this name, which in Babylonia and Assyria became a generic term simply meaning 'god', to the Arabian *Ilāh* familiar to us in the form *Allāh*, which is compounded of *al*, the definite article, and *Ilāh* by eliding the vowel 'i', is not clear. Some scholars trace the name to the South Arabian *Ilāh*, a title of the Moon god, but this is a matter of antiquarian interest. In Arabia Allāh was known from Christian and Jewish sources as the one god, and there can be no doubt whatever that he was known to the pagan Arabs of Mecca as the supreme being. Were this not so, the Qurān would have been unintelligible to the Meccans; moreover, it is clear from Nabataean and other inscriptions that Allāh meant 'the god'.

The other gods mentioned in the Qurān are all female deities:[1] Al-Lāt, al-ʿUzzā, and Manāt, which represented the Sun, the planet Venus, and Fortune, respectively; at Mecca they were regarded as daughters of Allāh. The cult of Al-Lāt was widespread. As Allāh means 'the god', so Al-Lāt means 'the goddess'. She is mentioned by Herodotus; in old Arabian inscriptions; and in the pre-Islamic poets; and was the great mother goddess who, under various names, was worshipped all over the ancient world. Tā'if, a town near Mecca, was a centre of her worship. For the Meccans al-ʿUzzā, 'the mighty one', was the most important. Evidence for her wor-

---

1. The five gods mentioned in sūra 71:22 need not be discussed here, but the verse is a valuable witness to the number of gods with whom the Meccans were familiar.

ship from the fourth century A.D. onwards is copious. Tradition says that in his youth Muhammad sacrificed a white sheep to her. When Muhammad took up arms against the pagans of Mecca, the latter took into battle images of Al-Lāt and al-'Uzzā, and their battle-cry, 'Strength is ours, you have no strength' ('izza), was probably a taunt in reply to the Prophet's assertion that these gods had no real existence but were merely names which they and their forefathers had invented. Manāt was a goddess of a different type who controlled the community's fortunes. All through Arabic literature there runs the thought of time the destroyer (the forerunner of Allāh's decree), which settles man's fate, strive how he will, and Manāt seems to be a deified representative of the all-pervading mystery of life and death. She was sometimes a household deity.

The heathenism with which Muhammad came to grips was largely animistic in nature and similar in many respects to the most primitive form of religion in the Old Testament. Like the Old Testament prophets, Muhammad took steps to put an end to practices which were inconsistent with monotheism. Idols, that is to say images fashioned by hand, were probably brought into Arabia from the surrounding countries, or made from foreign models. These were systematically destroyed by missions dispatched by the Prophet himself for that purpose. The primitive worship of the Arabs was given to the god or spirit who was believed to inhabit blocks of stone, rocks, trees, or wells. These stones served as altars and the blood of the victims was smeared or poured on them while the tribesmen danced round the stone. Herodotus states very credibly that blood-brotherhood was established in this way. The devotees licked the blood, or dipped their hands in it, and thus a reciprocal bond held them to one another and the deity to whom the stone belonged. Nilus, a Christian writer, gives a fairly full account of such a sacrifice to 'Uzzā. Though there is no trace of human sacrifice in the Qurān, it is clear from the authority just quoted and from early Arab sources that human beings were sacrificed to these gods in Dūma and Hīra.

The Qurān condemns the heathen rites as sacred stones, which it calls uncleanness and the work of Satan. It orders believers to have nothing to do with them, and forbids Muslims to eat the meat of an animal which has been slain at such a place. Gods were honoured by a kiss, or by stroking the rock or stone with the hand, the underlying idea being that the worshipper would acquire holiness by contagion. This is one of the practices which will be described later in connexion with the ceremonies of the *hajj* or pilgrimage; but it is worth noticing here that there is a tradition that the Caliph 'Umar once said of the Black Stone which is kissed by the pilgrims, 'Had I not seen the Prophet kiss you, I would not kiss you myself.'

Trees were also regarded as sacred because a deity inhabited them, and the practice of hanging scraps of clothing, rags, and other personal belongings on the branches of a sacred tree persists to this day in country districts in the Near East, and much the same may be said of the cult of wells and springs. All these beliefs and customs are inconsistent with monotheism, but neither Christianity nor Judaism has succeeded in extirpating them entirely, so it need not surprise us if Islam has not been more successful.

Like the early Hebrews, the Arabs appear to have had no conception of a resurrection: at any rate it is clear from the Qurān that Muhammad's teaching of a physical resurrection was received with incredulity and ridicule; nevertheless, there must have been some belief in some quarters in a shadowy existence after death similar to the early Hebrew belief in Sheol, where the dead lived on in the gloom and darkness of the under-world conscious of their surroundings. In many parts of the world at a certain stage of cultural development it was the custom to provide the dead man with the means of life to which he was accustomed. He was given food, cooking pots, a horse, and sometimes servants to attend to his wants in the future life. It is extremely unlikely that the Arabs went as far as this, but if we may believe the statements of later Arab writers, a she-camel was tethered and left to die by the dead man's grave, the idea being that he would one day ride her again. The apostolic tradition of Islam condemns all such practices.

Temples were few and far between. Outside the famous sanctuary of the Ka'ba at Mecca there was a Ka'ba in Nejrān on the Sa'ūdī-Yaman border (discovered by Mr Philby in 1936[1]) and one at San'ā. In these last two places Christian cathedrals once stood. Doubtless the extraordinary pains that were taken in their construction and decoration were directed towards weaning the pagan population from their agelong practices. In addition to these there were many sanctuaries served by priests who dwelt within their inviolate confines. The titles of many of the early Meccans indicate that the Ka'ba itself was given great honour. How the Prophet dealt with his ancestral sanctuary will be shown later.

2. JEWS

We do not know when Jews first settled in Arabia. There are three obvious possibilities: (a) the eighth, (b) the sixth cen-

1. St John Philby, *Arabian Highlands*, 1952, pp. 220 f.

tury B.C., and (c) the first and second centuries A.D. (a) The first date would connect the Jewish community in Arabia with the fall of Samaria in 721 B.C. This is not so improbable as it sounds, since it is almost certain that the self-contained Jewish military colony in Aswān in upper Egypt, about which the world knew nothing until a few years ago, was founded just after the fall of Samaria, and consequently it is not impossible that some Jewish settlements in Arabia were due to fugitives fleeing from the old northern capital of the Hebrews. (b) The second date marks a much greater dispersion, when the large Jewish settlements in Mesopotamia which have survived to the present day were founded. (c) The last date is perhaps the most probable, because the Romans were so utterly ruthless in their repression of the Jews that few dared remain in Palestine, and Arabia offered a near asylum. The presence of Jews on the trade route from South to North Arabia is well attested in the Greco-Roman age. It is of course possible that homeless Jews or their enterprising merchant colonists entered Arabia from the eighth century B.C. onwards until the rise of Islam.

There was a large Jewish colony in the Yaman in pre-Islamic times, and they maintained an organized communal existence for centuries until they were brought to Palestine a few years ago. These Yamanite Jews certainly go back to the fourth century A.D., and at one time the ruling king had become a Jew. Two descendants of these people exercised a profound influence on Muslim tradition.

At the dawn of Islam the Jews dominated the economic life of the Hijaz. They held all the best land in the oases of Taimā', Fadak, and Wādi-l-Qurā; at Medina they must have formed at least half of the population. There was also a Jewish settlement to the north of the Gulf of 'Aqaba. In the Hijaz have been found Jewish tombs dating from the second and third centuries. These may well be brought into connexion with the statement of an Arab writer that when the Romans conquered Palestine bands of Jewish refugees fled to the Hijāz. Whether this writer is referring to the destruction of Jerusalem by Titus in A.D. 70, or to the savage reprisals which followed the revolt of Bar Kokba in 136, cannot be determined, nor is the point important. What is important is to note that the Jews of the Hijāz made many proselytes among the Arab tribesmen.

The prosperity of the Jews was due to their superior knowledge of agriculture and irrigation and their energy and industry. Homeless refugees in the course of a few generations became large landowners in the country, controllers of its finance and trade. Apparently they 'cornered' the iron trade, for it was they who supplied arms, coats of mail, and agricultural implements to their neighbours for a suitable consideration. At Taymā' a Jew named Samuel controlled the fair to which the tribesmen came to buy and sell and to barter their women's woven work for arms and such rough tools as they needed, while at Medina the market was controlled by a Jewish tribe. Thus it can readily be seen that Jewish prosperity was a challenge to the Arabs, particularly the Quraysh at Mecca and the Aus and Khazraj at Medina. To the former tribe Muhammad himself belonged, while his supporters at Medina, to whom he was related by blood, belonged to the latter two tribes. When the Muslims took up arms they treated the Jews with much greater severity than the Christians, who, until the end of the purely Arab Caliphate, were not badly treated. The most probable reasons for this discrimination are (a) the Arabs' resentment of their economic exploitation by the Jews, and (b) the Qurān's scornful words.

In the nature of things there is no need to give an account of Judaism. Everyone is familiar with its main tenets, though some stories which were current in what is called *midrash*, that is to say allegorical and sometimes fanciful explanations of scripture stories and Rabbinical tradition which have found their way into the Qurān, will not be familiar to the general reader.

3. CHRISTIANS

If we use the word Arabian in its widest sense, Arabian Christianity is as old as Christianity itself. In Damascus the place where St Paul was let down from the wall in a basket is still shown to visitors, and tradition associates the apostle St Thomas with the founding of the church at Edessa in Iraq. One would not suppose from reading the Qurān that an enormous number of Arabs were Christians. Though the bedouin of the Hijāz were predominantly pagan, many of the surrounding tribes had accepted Christianity, either whole-heartedly or as a matter of form. Apart from scattered Christian communities throughout the Arabian peninsula the three chief centres of influence were the Yaman in the south, Syria in the north, and Hīra in the east. (Abyssinia, to which some of Muhammad's companions were forced to flee, was Christian in communion with the Egyptian Monophysite church.) The Hijāz was invaded from the Yaman by the Christian general Abraha *c.* A.D. 570. The sūra called *The Elephant* refers to this. In the Hijāz itself there were at least two Christian tribes, Judham and 'Udhra. In Mecca we hear only of individual Christians, though it is to be noted that they belonged to Quraysh. Tradition mentions a few others. It is credibly recorded that when Muhammad entered Mecca in triumph in the year 630, paintings of Jesus and the Virgin Mary, among others, were still visible on the inner walls of the Ka'ba. He ordered all the paintings except that of the Virgin and Child to be expunged; this painting was seen by an eye-witness as late as 683, when so much of the Ka'ba was destroyed by fire that it had to be rebuilt.

An incidental indication of the presence of Christians in the Hijāz is to be found in the tradition which records that Muhammad wore tunics which had been given him by monks in the neighbouring desert.

As we shall see, when Muhammad reached manhood, Arab Christianity was split into rival camps weakened by persecutions and internecine war, and filled with utter detestation of the Greeks. The Arab Christians were drawn into quarrels with which they had little sympathy, though they displayed that loyalty to leaders who had won their respect and confidence which has always been a mark of the Arab people.

The old divisions of Arab Christianity – Greek Orthodox, Monophysite (Jacobite), and Nestorian – still survive to this day, though in much reduced numbers and in vastly different proportions. Of the first it is unnecessary to speak; the Monophysites held that there was only one nature in Christ who was the divine Word (notice the expression 'a word from Him' used to explain the office of Jesus in the Qurān) incarnate. Nestorians held that Christ was truly man but was born as God of the Virgin Mary, uniting in himself two natures. Christology is such an extremely complicated and technical subject that few but professional theologians can understand the niceties of the disputes, and no more need be said of it here.

The Monophysites were extraordinarily active in converting the Arabs, and shortly before the birth of Muhammad large numbers had been baptized. A priest and deacon were appointed to each tribe. Churches were founded, almsgiving and fasting were regularly practised. Monasteries were open day and night to travellers, who were given food and drink before they were sent on their way. Women were veiled when out of doors.

The Nestorians were equally active. They established schools in many towns. In their monasteries monks could be heard chanting their offices, so that the Arabs became accustomed to seeing the monks at prayer day and night, prostrating themselves with their faces to the ground. In prayer the Christians turned to the east. Such men were a familiar sight on all the caravan routes of Arabia. The monastery at Hīra was established by the Nestorians in the fifth century, and from thence Christianity was carried to Bahrayn. While Muhammad was a young man, King Nuʿmān of Hīra was converted to Christianity. The church in the east was predominantly Nestorian, though a fair number of Monophysites were to be found there.

The eastern and the western Arabs were continually at war because they were hired as mercenaries by the Persians and Greeks respectively. The former, who had their base at Hīra near Kūfa, are known as the Lakhmids, while the latter moved round Damascus and are known as the Ghassānids. As the Arabs from time immemorial have been given to raiding, this division suited them admirably, and they fought for their overlords with courage and determination; but both empires made the same mistake: they withdrew their subsidies and treacherously murdered or imprisoned the Arab kings, and so turned their most valuable auxiliaries into enemies thirsting for vengeance. Chosroes II murdered the

Christian king Nu'mān, and the eastern Arabs everywhere were in revolt. While Muhammad was preaching at Mecca the Christian Arabs destroyed a considerable force of Persians to avenge the death of their leader, and they were constantly raiding Persian territory until the advent of the Muslim armies from the Hijāz gave them the chance to settle their account with the Persians once and for all.

As we shall see, the march of events on the other side of the desert was very similar, except that here religious persecution was much more prevalent and much more violent. From the sixth century onwards the history of the Arab west is one long series of persecutions in the name of orthodoxy, culminating in the alienation of the Arabs and the downfall of the Greek empire in Syria. As Monophysites the Arabs steadily refused to accept the doctrine of two natures in Christ. The persecutions which these unhappy people suffered were sometimes worse than their treatment by the Muslims in subsequent years. Bishops were driven from their sees, monks were expelled from their monasteries, ordinary laymen were driven from their homes and fled to Persian territory. Those who could not escape were imprisoned and tortured and not allowed to return to their homes. Even women and children were not exempt from these cruel assaults, and thousands died from starvation and exposure.

The famous Arab chief Hārith went to Constantinople to see the Emperor and to ask that his people might be given a Monophysite bishop, and as he was a valuable man at the head of the vassal tribes, Justinian I acceded to his wish. Consequently when the Persian Arabs, some ten years later, invaded Syria, Hārith attacked them so vigorously that they were driven off with great loss and their leader was killed. In 563 he went to see the Emperor again, carrying a letter which shows plainly how the way was being prepared for Islam. One sentence reads: 'The Trinity is one Divinity, one Nature, one Essence; those who will not accept this doctrine are to be anathematized.' When two bishops refused to sign the declaration of faith he brought, Hārith replied with the ominous words: 'Now I know that you are heretics. We and our armies accept this doctrine, as do the orientals.' Here plainly is a claim to a native Arab Christianity stripped of the subtle refinements of the Greek theologians, and an explicit claim to the right to defend that faith by the sword.

After the death of Hārith, his son Mundhir assumed the role of protector of the Monophysite Christians. He was a brave warrior and reduced the Persian Arabs to impotence in two campaigns. Conscious of the service he had rendered to the Greeks, Mundhir wrote to the Emperor asking for money to pay his tribes. He received an insulting refusal. Worse was to follow: by a mistake he received a letter intended for the Greek commander-in-chief who was fighting the Persians at the time, in which the latter was ordered to invite him to a conference and then kill him. As a result Mundhir withdrew his support from the Greeks and declared his independence. However, when the Greeks were defeated he could not look on while the Persians plundered his fellow Christians in Syria, and once again he agreed to fight on the side of the Greeks. By a surprise attack he annihilated the enemy's headquarters at Hīra. He cut to pieces the Arab force in the pay of the Persians and burnt the town to the ground, saving only the churches, and returned to Syria with enormous booty.

It would take us too far afield to follow the miserable course of religious controversy in the Arab world; suffice it to say that the Arab king showed himself a loyal friend to his bishop and tried his utmost to heal the breach in Christianity which kept his countrymen at one another's throats. He went to the Emperor in 580 to plead with him to put a stop to the disputes which were ruining Christianity among the Arabs, and he begged for charity and tolerance. The Emperor received him with great honour, and, assured of his support, called together the quarrelsome clergy and got them to agree to live in peace one with another. However, religious fanaticism soon broke out again. The clergy broke their word and persecutions and anathemas followed everywhere.

The end of this noble Arab was tragic. In the name of religion a false friend induced him to visit him without an armed guard, accused him of treachery, and took him in chains to Constantinople. At this the Arabs were thoroughly roused; they plundered the countryside in all directions in revenge for the ingratitude shown to their king. From this time forward their hatred of the Greeks knew no bounds. Mundhir's son Nu'mān swore that he would never look upon a Greek again, but he himself fell into Greek hands and was exiled to Sicily with his father. The old writer says: 'The kingdom of the Arabs was divided among fifteen princes; most of them joined forces with the Persians, and from this time onwards the rule of the Christian Arabs came to an end because of the treachery of the Greeks, and heresy was widespread amongst the Arabs.' By this time Muhammad was fast approaching manhood.

Thus the Greeks paved the way for their own downfall. Within a century or so Muslim Arabs were at the gates of Constantinople, and its ultimate fall to the Turks in 1453 was the logical outcome of the shameful treatment of the Arab Christians by their orthodox rulers. Their policy was as foolish as it was wicked. Henceforth they stood for tyranny and injustice in the eyes of the Arabs, and through them Christianity was associated with perfidy.

The Persians exploited the situation right up to the hijra. They got possession of Syria for years. Here they left the Arabs in comparative peace, but they killed all the Greeks they could lay their hands on. We need not doubt that the Christian Arabs who had gone over to them took every opportunity to avenge themselves on their persecutors. The Greeks came back in time to expel the Persians and meet the Muslim onslaught, but we are not surprised to read that when the Muslim general told the people of Hims and Damascus that he had come to deliver them from the Greeks, he was welcomed as a liberator.

The amazing rapidity of the Arab advance east and west to which all writers refer was due to the co-operation of the local Christians disgusted with Byzantine cruelty and oppression. All the Arabs had to do was to defeat a number of disaffected garrison troops; and this was comparatively easy, because in Syria the population welcomed them and joined forces with them, while in Egypt they made a separate peace, stipulating that the power of Byzantium must be irrevocably destroyed. It was not until the Muslim Arabs came up against native opposition farther west that they met with a serious check. In Egypt and the Arab world they were accepted as deliverers.

CHAPTER TWO

MUHAMMAD

IN writing of a man who is loved and venerated by millions of the world's citizens today, one would wish to be purely objective. So far as the greatest monument to Muhammad's memory – the Qurān – is concerned, that is not difficult; but his biography is much more difficult to deal with. To translate without comment the statements of his biographers without historical criticism would be misleading; on the other hand, to generalize as some Western scholars have done would be rash. No unprejudiced scholar doubts that legend has been active in the Arabic biographies and traditions, where the prophet is sometimes portrayed as writers think he should have been rather than as he was. This subject will be considered further in chapter 6.

However, the brief sketch of Muhammad that follows is an attempt to set forth his life history as a prophet and as the greatest statesman of his time, leaving it to speak for itself. By a happy chance a great Arab writer of the fourteenth century, Ibn Khaldūn, whose disquisition on the philosophy of history has long been recognized as of permanent value, has written some penetrating paragraphs on the criticism of traditional history which will serve as a guide to historical research.

Since it is of the nature of tradition to incorporate false statements we must examine the causes which produce them. They are:

(*a*) attachment to certain opinions and schools of thought. Now if a man's mind is impartial in receiving tradition he examines it with all due care so that he can distinguish between the true and the false; but if he is pervaded by attachment to any particular opinion or sect he immediately accepts any tradition which supports it; and this tendency and attachment cloud his judgement so that he is unable to criticize and scrutinize what he hears, and straightway accepts what is false and hands it on to others;

(*b*) over-confidence in the probity of those who hand on the tradition;

(*c*) ignorance of the real significance of events; for many traditionists, now knowing the significance of what they saw and heard, record events together with their own interpretations or conjectures and so give false information;

(*d*) belief that one has the truth. This is widespread and comes generally from over-confidence in narrators of the past;

(*e*) ignorance of the circumstances surrounding an event induced by ambiguity or embellishment. The narrator hands on the story as he understands it with these misleading and false elements.

As every unprejudiced observer knows, these faults are not peculiar to Muslim Arab writers: they are a feature of most hagiographies. Let us take but one example from the earliest biography of Muhammad, that of Ibn Ishāq who died in A.H. 150, and compare it with a similar story in the Old Testament. The occasion is the threat of Abraha, the Abyssinian general, to occupy Mecca. A small contingent of elephants made a deep impression on the Arabs, and Abraha's force easily defeated the tribes who opposed their advance. 'Abd al-Muttalib, the prophet's grandfather, knowing that effective resistance to the Abyssinian army was impossible, called upon Allah to defend his sanctuary, and betook himself to the surrounding hills. Meanwhile a virulent attack of smallpox broke out in the enemy's ranks, and they were forced to withdraw, hundreds of them dying by the wayside as they returned to the south. These are the facts. But Arab legend has imported a miraculous element into the story: Allāh sent flocks of birds which dropped on the enemy three small stones; each bird carried two stones in its claws and one in its beak, and every Abyssinian who was hit by the stones perished. This account is canonized in sūra 105: 'Have you not considered how your Lord dealt with the army of the elephant? Did he not bring their schemes to nought? He sent flocks of birds against them which rained clay pellets upon them so that they became like grass which cattle have eaten.' The point of the legend is that Mecca, the sanctuary founded by Abraham, is God's house, and that He miraculously saves it from violation.

Somewhat similar is the story of the annihilation of the Assyrian army led by Sennacherib against Jerusalem, also the sanctuary of God. An overwhelming force of Assyrians threaten the city and Hezekiah, unable to resist, calls upon God to deliver the city. The prophet Isaiah predicts that God will defend Jerusalem and that Sennacherib will be forced to return by the way he came. That night the angel of the Lord smote the Assyrians and 185,000 of them perished. The Greek historian Herodotus says that field-mice gnawed the bowstrings and shield-thongs of the soldiers during the night and the army had to withdraw. Mice were a symbol of pestilence. In both these legends we have an example of the way in which epidemics were 'explained' in the pre-scientific age. There was no understanding of cause and effect: everything was due to the immediate operation of God himself, and some small living creature was thought to be his instrument in bringing disease on mankind.

Into the same category fall the stories of mysterious lights and portents in the heavens which are to be found in hagiologies. They are not history, but are stories invented to glorify the memory of men who are revered as God's messengers to men. They are not of the essence of religion. A prophet's personality should be able to stand on its own merits. If it can, it needs no portent; if it cannot, a portent merely compromises the credibility of the whole narrative by importing the incredible.

Accordingly, the life of Muhammad freed from these well-meant but unintelligent accretions must be left to speak for itself. Anyone who wishes to understand the position of the pious Muslim ought to remember how deeply the Christmas story of the star 'which stood over where the young child was' is rooted in the hearts and affections of Christians. If similar stories appear in the biography of Muhammad they should be regarded with sympathy and understanding. Whether they are historically true or not is comparatively unimportant. In passing it ought to be observed that the narrator often says 'it is asserted that', or 'as they say', which is sufficient indication of his attitude towards some of the pious legends he puts on record.

At the outset let it be said that Muhammad was one of the great figures of history whose overmastering conviction was that there was one God alone and that there should be one community of believers. His ability as a statesman faced with problems of extraordinary complexity is truly amazing. With all the power of armies, police, and civil service no Arab has ever succeeded in holding his countrymen together as he did. If it is objected that the Muslim territory and population at his death was vastly less than that of the empire of the Caliphs, it may be replied that all the elements of disunion were present in his lifetime but dared not show themselves until his death became known.

Muhammad was born in Mecca about the year A.D. 570. The first absolutely certain date in his life is that on which the Muhammadan era is based, the hijra, i.e. the migration from

Mecca to Medina, about 280 miles to the north-east, in 622. We know, too, that his prophetic activity in Mecca before that date lasted more than ten years, and he is said to have been 40 or, according to other authorities, 43 years old at his call. He was the posthumous son of 'Abd Allāh and the grandson of the 'Abd al-Muttalib mentioned above, whose father was Hāshim, the name still borne by the royal families of Iraq and Jordan. Hāshim had married a woman of Medina who belonged to the clan of 'Adī ibn al-Najjār which formed part of the tribe of Khazraj, and thus Muhammad had blood ties with Medina. Mecca was held by the tribe of Quraysh, and Muhammad belonged to a well-established but impoverished family there. It is clear from sūra 43:30, '[The Unbelievers] say, Why was this Qurān not revealed to a great man in the two towns?' that when that was written Muhammad himself was not a person of great standing. Therefore his subsequent success must be accounted the greater in that he converted his opponents without the help which prestige and a high social position would have given him. His mother died when he was still a little boy, and he was brought up by his grandfather, a kindly, generous, and stout-hearted man who lived and died a pagan; and then by his uncle Abū Tālib. Very little is known of Muhammad's childhood. A foster-mother was found for him among the Banū Sa'd. After he had sojourned with them more than two years he received a supernatural visitation which is described by his foster-mother Halīma thus: 'His brother came running to us saying, "Two men in white garments seized my Qurayshite brother, knocked him down, split his belly open, and are stirring it up!" We went to him and found him standing erect, his countenance pale and wan. When we asked him what had happened he said exactly what his brother had said, adding that he did not know what the two men were searching for in his belly. My husband said that he feared that he was afflicted and that I must take him back to his people before the malady became apparent to all. This I did, and in answer to a direct question from his mother I admitted that I thought that he was possessed by a devil, but she told me that my fears were groundless and of the wonderful circumstances of his birth.' Exactly what lies behind this story of the opening and cleansing of Muhammad's belly it is hard to see, unless it is an attempt to give a literal meaning to the metaphorical statement in the Qurān, 'Did we not open thy breast for thee?' (93:1). It is worth noticing that later writers place the incident in Muhammad's later manhood, immediately before his ascension to heaven.

A past generation of Arabists, on the basis of this tradition and accounts of the symptoms of physical distress which sometimes accompanied his utterances, advanced the theory that Muhammad was an epileptic. The charge had been made by a Byzantine writer long before. Such a hypothesis seems gratuitous, and can safely be ascribed to anti-Muhammadan prejudice. Study of the psychological phenomena of religious experience makes it extremely improbable. Prophets are not normal people, but that does not authorize the assertion that their abnormal behaviour is due to a morbid condition. Moreover, Muhammad was a man whose common sense never failed him. Those who deny his mental and psychic stability do so only by ignoring the overwhelming evidence of his shrewd appraisal of others and of the significance of what was going on in the world of his time, and his persistence in the face of constant opposition until he united his people in the religion of Islam. Had he ever collapsed in the strain of battle or controversy, or fainted away when strong action was called for, a case might be made out. But all the evidence we have points in the opposite direction, and the suggestion of epilepsy is as groundless in the eyes of the present writer as it is offensive to all Muslims. It may be added that most modern writers, as opposed to those of the last generation, are of this opinion. To base such a theory on a legend which on the face of it has no historical foundation is a sin against historical criticism.

The only authentic story of Muhammad's early years is contained in an unpublished manuscript of his first biographer Ibn Ishāq. It reads as follows:

I was told that the apostle of Allah said, as he was talking about Zayd son of 'Amr son of Nufayl, 'He was the first to upbraid me for idolatry and forbade me to worship idols. I had come from al-Tā'if along with Zayd son of Hāritha when we passed Zayd son of 'Amr who was in the highland of Mecca. Quraysh had made a public example of him for abandoning their religion, so that he went out from their midst. I sat down with him. I had a bag containing meat which we had sacrificed to our idols – Zayd b. Hāritha was carrying it – and I offered it to Zayd b. 'Amr – I was but a lad at the time – and I said. "Eat some of this food, my uncle." He replied, "Surely it is part of those sacrifices of theirs which they offer to their idols?" When I said that it was, he said, "Nephew mine, if you were to ask the daughters of 'Abd al-Muttalib they would tell you that I never eat of these sacrifices, and I have no desire to do so." Then he upbraided me for idolatry and spoke disparagingly of those who worship idols and sacrifice to them, and said, "They are worthless: they can neither harm nor profit anyone," or words to that effect.' The apostle added, 'After that I never knowingly stroked one of their idols nor did I sacrifice to them until God honoured me with his apostleship.'

This tradition clearly shows how the boy Muhammad was influenced by a monotheist of whom we know but little. The prohibition against the eating of meat offered to idols is of course originally Jewish, but as it was taken over into Christianity it is impossible to say whether Zayd was a Jewish or a Christian proselyte. Arabic tradition represents him as a man dissatisfied with both Judaism and Christianity and utterly hostile to heathenism.

At the age of 25, after being employed by a wealthy widow to look after her camels trading with Damascus, Muhammad so impressed her by his person and abilities that she proposed marriage. She was fifteen years his senior. Their married life was happy, and she bore him two sons and four daughters. The boys died in infancy. His daughters married as follows: Zaynab married Abu'l-ʿĀs; Ruqayya married ʿUthmān who became the third Caliph; Fātima married ʿAlī; and Umm Kulthūm married ʿUtayba. Of these the marriage of Fātima to ʿAlī was of lasting importance, for it is in this line that the prophet's descendants are specially revered, and the Shīʿas look upon the descendants of ʿAlī and Fātima as the true heirs to the Caliphate, with all the religious and secular privileges pertaining to that office.

Two words are applied to him, namely *nabī*, prophet, and *rasūl*, one who is sent, i.e. an apostle. The first has a long history in Judaism and Christianity, beginning with Saul, c. 1000 B.C. and ending some time after the Christian era; the second, though known to the Jews by name, is in essence a Christian term, applied to a man sent by God.

Among other Semitic peoples there were men who foretold the future, announced the will of the gods, gave oracles, and so on; but the Hebrew religion gave content and meaning to the word *nabī* which, originally applied to a person who in a state of uncontrollable emotion and excitement proclaimed a message which his hearers attributed to a god, afterwards became the title of the preachers of monotheism and social justice. Among the pagan Arabs there could not be a *nabī*, as there was no definite conception of such a God, but there were men who discharged some of the functions of the *nabī*, namely the *shā'irs* (literally 'knowers'), i.e. men with a mysterious esoteric knowledge which was generally attributed to a familiar spirit called a *jinnī* or *shaytān*. *Shā'ir* later came to mean 'poet', for the reason that these men in their ominous predictions used a rhymed prose in which a rough rhythm was preserved.

The outward marks of a prophet in Israel were (*a*) impassioned utterance; (*b*) poetry; (*c*) intense preoccupation with God and moral issues; (*d*) a sense of compulsion urging him to declare the will of God. Naturally these characteristics varied from prophet to prophet: in some of the later prophets the feeling of excitement, the inner urge which bursts as it were the bounds of language, and the idealism are altogether lacking; but the broad pattern is consistent. How far then is it possible to say that Muhammad was a prophet?

Now if we look at the accounts of his call, as recorded by the early biographers, some very interesting parallels with Hebrew prophets come to light. They say that it was his habit to leave the haunts of men and retire to the mountains to give himself up to prayer and meditation. One night as he was asleep the angel Gabriel came to him with a piece of silk brocade whereon words were written, and said 'Recite!' He answered, 'What shall I recite?' The order was repeated three times, while he felt continually increasing physical pressure, until the angel said:

> Recite in the name of thy Lord who created
> Man from blood coagulated.

Recite! Thy Lord is wondrous kind
Who by the pen has taught mankind
Things they knew not (being blind).[1]

When he woke these words seemed to be written on his heart (or, as we should say, impressed indelibly on his mind). Then the thought came to him that he must be a *shāʿir* or possessed, he who had so hated such people that he could not bear the sight of them; and he could not tolerate the thought that his tribesmen would regard him as one of them – as in fact they afterwards did. Thereupon he left the place with the intention of throwing himself over a precipice. But while on his way he heard a voice from heaven hailing him as the Apostle of God, and lifting up his eyes he saw a figure astride the horizon which turned him from his purpose and kept him rooted to the spot. And there he remained long after his anxious wife's messengers had returned to report that they could not find him.

Clearly this story belongs to the realm of visions and dreams. Whatever view is taken of their objective reality, none can doubt their subjective reality to those who experience them. This inaugural vision so affected Muhammad's preaching – at any rate in its early stages – and Muhammad himself, that it is possible to believe that he was a prophet. The burden of Muhammad's message from first to last was the almighty power of God and man's duty to obey him, of sin and judgement. The sense of compulsion under which he laboured is clearly brought out in the dream in which the angel forced him to speak. Some of his biographers have deleted the passages which speak of his doubts and fears; but they are perhaps the most convincing elements in the story, and, apart from his contemplated suicide, are strongly

1. A rough attempt is made to reproduce the rhyme.

reminiscent of Jeremiah's doubts as to whether he was inspired or whether he was on the same level as the false prophets of his day. And as we shall see, Muhammad's tenacity was tested by adversity – mockery, accusations of soothsaying and of teaching the doctrines of foreigners, and finally undisguised persecution. His biographer says truly that prophethood is a weighty and painful office which few can sustain owing to the opposition that they encounter.

Unfortunately very little is known about the prophet's life during the fifteen years which intervened between his marriage and his call. What was going on in his mind? Whom did he meet who could impart information about Judaism and Christianity whose scriptures he claimed to confirm or correct? Tradition asserts that as a boy of 12, while travelling to Syria with his uncle Abū Ṭālib, he met a monk called Bahīra who hailed him as God's messenger, and one would suppose he must often have taken the same route into a Christian country when in charge of Khadīja's caravans, though there are no specific statements to that effect. We have seen how the whole area was permeated by converts to the two monotheistic religions. It would be unthinkable that a man dissatisfied with the religion of his people and earnestly seeking divine guidance should not endeavour to acquaint himself with the religion of those who claimed to worship the only true God. One of the most significant verses in the Qurān (10:94) on this subject reads: 'If thou art in doubt about anything that We have revealed to thee, ask those who read the scriptures before thee.'

Th vision was followed by a period not unlike that which Western mystics have called 'the dark night of the soul', during which the mind and body exhausted by trances and

visions suffer from depression and lassitude, and doubts pre-
vail.

During this pause Muhammad was sustained by his wife's
faith and support, and after a time fresh messages came to
him, culminating in the command to proclaim publicly what
he had been taught. No doubt he drew comfort from reflecting on the sadness of his early life and the goodness of God,
who had rescued him from poverty and sustained him in
adversity until relief came. Sūra 93 is a touching soliloquy
on this period:

> Did He not find thee an orphan and give thee a home?
> Did He not find thee in error and guide thee to the truth?

Error and true guidance in later chapters of the Qurān normally refer to the way of life pursued by polytheists and
believers respectively.

At first conversions were made secretly, until the tiny
community's habit of daily prayer became known to the
Meccans, who began to mock and finally to take steps to put
an end to a movement which threatened their position as the
hereditary possessors of a venerated sanctuary of the gods and
the wealth which they drew from the annual pilgrimages to
the Ka'ba. One is reminded of the first preaching of Christianity at Ephesus, where the silversmiths complained that
'this man Paul has persuaded and turned away much people,
saying that they are not gods which are made with hands,
and not only is there danger that this trade of ours may come
into disrepute, but also that the temple of the great goddess
Artemis will be made of no account, and that she will even
be deposed from her magnificence, she whom all Asia and
the world worships.'[1] The Meccans were not to know that

1. Acts 19:26.

when the struggle between them and Muhammad was over Mecca would remain as the sanctuary of Allāh to which all Muslims must resort at least once in their lives.

In a later generation it was of great moment to determine who was the first man to accept Islam. The rival candidates are Abū Bakr, the first caliph, Muhammad's faithful friend and subsequent father-in-law, and his cousin and afterwards son-in-law, 'Alī. It is almost certain that the honour belongs to Abū Bakr, and that 'Alī's name has been put forward by the Shī'a with whom Ibn Ishāq the early biographer undoubtedly sympathized. Except for dynastic and political reasons the point is of no importance, because admittedly 'Alī was a child at the time, while the adherence of a well-to-do merchant, popular and respected, was of enormous value to Muhammad. Abū Bakr remained his devoted friend to the end of his life, sharing his exile, and rejoicing in his success. Whatever accusations of self-interest may be levelled against later converts when it was highly profitable to be a Muslim, there can be no doubt that Abū Bakr accepted Muhammad as a divinely sent leader when he was despised and insulted by his fellow townsmen. Muhammad possessed abundantly the gift of evoking loyalty and affection from men. The proud title of 'Companions' (Ashāb) is given to those who were his early associates; 'Exiles' (muhājirūn) to those who shared his flight to Medina; and 'Helpers' (Ansār) to the men of Medina. Thus Muslims have recognized not merely the importance of these men in that they could hand on to future generations traditions of what their master had said and done, but also that they were men who believed in him and helped him before he rose to power when it was not in their interest to do so.

The majority of Muhammad's early converts were slaves

or people of humble origin, though a few of the leading merchants of Mecca accepted Islam. History teaches us that any religious reformer who is determined to overthrow the existing order of society is bound to meet with the opposition of those whose interests are threatened by his innovations. Parties who enjoy financial, ecclesiastical, and social advantages from an established religion will not forego those privileges without a struggle, and in the last resort are prepared to kill the man who attacks them. From the Qurān one can see the very real fear of the Meccans that the destruction of the gods would lead to their downfall; that if Muhammad succeeded in converting the majority of the townsfolk he would inevitably become their leader and they would lose their position as heads of the community. If Allāh really wanted to send a message why did he not choose one of themselves? As he had not done so, clearly Muhammad was an impostor. Are we to believe in one whom the dregs of the people follow? It is wealth that he is really seeking!

In the early stages of the conflict the Meccans tried to discredit Muhammad by ridicule and accusations of sorcery, and finally of downright fraud in that he got his ideas from a foreigner – some Jew or Christian – with whom he conversed daily. All these charges, which are denied in the Qurān, are dealt with at greater length in the biographies, which generally suffer from overstatement and exaggeration. Furthermore, if he really was the prophet of God why did he bring no sign to confirm his statements? Muhammad's answer was that the Qurān with its inimitable language was itself the sign he brought. After a time the position of his followers became so intolerable that nearly a hundred of them were forced to migrate to Abyssinia to take refuge with the Christians there, and possibly it was about this time the prophet said in the Qurān that 'You will find the most affectionate friends will be those who say, "We are Christians".' The refugees were well treated and given complete freedom to practise their religion as they desired.

This was a period of constant pinpricks, petty insults, and persecution of those who had no influential patron; in fact something like a boycott of the Muslims was put in force. Constant bickering and argument forced the prophet to state his position on several important matters which will be mentioned in the next chapter. The biographer relates many of the suras to these controversies. Naturally the battle between monotheism and polytheism could have only one ending, and gradually but surely the number of Muslims increased. The most important accession to their ranks was 'Umar, who has been called the St Paul of Islam. He was a man of courage – physical and moral – and once he had given his word he never thought of turning back. In after years he was one of the men whom the prophet always consulted, and his downright character often overawed his opponents who feared his violence.

During this period of waxing persecution Muhammad owed his immunity and possibly his life to the protection of his uncle Abū Tālib. A characteristic virtue of the Arabs has always been, and still is, an unflinching loyalty to members of their family, clan, or tribe. This shows itself in a readiness to protect them against their enemies, if necessary by their own lives. It is our boast that a slave is free when he reaches British soil, and that a political refugee is inviolate; but the Arabs go further. Any man who claims their protection is safe, and though modern States have extradition treaties with Arab lands, it would be unwise to count on their application in a Muslim country. Vendettas are disliked and men are chary of provoking them. For this reason a family or tribe will pay the fine inflicted by authority or the compensation demanded by an individual; but it will not hand over its own flesh and blood or its guest to the tender mercies of his enemy. The conception of law administered by the State is of course well known in the Muslim world, but it has never been allowed to override the innate conviction of the Arab that he and his are one. Thus fortified by explicit assurance and inner certainty of support against aggression Muhammad pursued his way.

Distressed by the estrangement from his townsmen and by the illwill that beset him, Muhammad was led into making a temporary but very small concession to heathenism. In sura 53:19 he recited the words: 'Al-Lat, al-'Uzzā, and Manāt are the exalted virgins [the exact meaning of the word is not known] whose intercession may be counted on.' These words immediately won over the Meccans who joined him in prostrating themselves before Allāh; but, as the biographer reports, Gabriel came to him and upbraided him for including words which had not been revealed to him, and revealed (sūra 22:51): 'Never have we sent apostle or prophet before you but when he allowed his own wishes to predominate Satan interjected [words] into his desires; but God cancels what Satan interjects.' Critics of tradition have endeavoured to discredit the honesty of those who reported this story; but it is impossible to suggest a motive for its invention other than a desire to discredit Muhammad, the Qurān, and Islam itself – and such a supposition in regard to sincere Muslims is absurd. In fact the incident is the strongest possible testimony to the sincerity of Muhammad. Of course it opens the door to the enquiry whether he may have been mistaken in supposing that his words were inspired on other

occasions also; but as the Qurān itself rightly says, this has
been the possible fate of prophets at all times, and there have
been prophets who have not frankly and immediately acknowledged that they were mistaken. Too much can be made
of this incident, which will be referred to again. All that these
interpolated words meant was that the divine or semi-divine
beings acted as intercessors with Allāh, an office which in
Islam is accorded only to Muhammad himself. Nevertheless
it was a declension from the prophet's doctrine of pure monotheism inasmuch as the next step would logically be prayer
and supplication to the guardian angels or heavenly intercessors; there is little in Sunnī Islam to warrant the supposition that there is any mediator between God and the believer.
The orthodox belief is that the prophet's intercession may be
hoped for on the day of resurrection. But to return to our
subject.

When Muhammad withdrew these words and asserted
that these goddesses had no reality but were mere names, the
Meccans were more angry than before. A crisis was approaching: death carried away his faithful wife Khadīja and
his protector Abū Tālib, and his townsmen remained hostile
and suspicious. The only thing to do was to look further
afield. Accordingly he made a beginning at Tā'if, a town
some sixty miles to the east and in close relations with Mecca.
He preached there for several days, but met with mockery
and insult. Young men hooted at him in the streets and
pelted him with stones, so that he was forced to flee bleeding
from cuts and bruises. Retiring to recuperate awhile in a vine-
yard outside the town he uttered the following prayer, which
may be left to speak for his sincerity and devotion:

O God, I complain to Thee of my weakness and insufficiency
and low estate in the sight of men. O most merciful One, Thou art

the Lord of the weak and Thou art my Lord. To whom wilt Thou entrust me? To strangers who will look askance at me or to enemies to whom Thou hast given power over me? If Thou art not angry with me I care not; but Thy defence is broader. I take refuge in the light of Thy countenance (at which the very darkness shines and the affairs of this world and the next are justly balanced), lest Thine anger should descend upon me or Thy wrath light upon me. It is for Thee to be satisfied until Thou art pleased. There is no power, no strength but in Thee.

Though this prayer does not rest upon a sound tradition according to Arabian standards, being introduced by the words 'among the things that I was told'; and though the style differs considerably from that of the Qurān, it may well have formed the substance of the prophet's intercession at this time. To suppose that someone stood by to commit to memory the exact words of the petition is as repugnant to common sense as to reverence and decency.

On the way back to Mecca a number of *jinn* or spirits are said to have jostled him in their eagerness to hear his prayers and eagerness to embrace Islam. Whether this is a memory of what the prophet told his friends afterwards, or whether it is a story written to explain the background of the sūra of the Jinn (72) and sūra 46:28 ff. is uncertain. But certainly the Qurān asserts that Muhammad preached to these creatures and converted them. More will be said on this subject in the next chapter.

Before he could re-enter Mecca Muhammad had to seek protection from al-Mut'im the son of 'Adī. Soon after he married a widow called Sauda, and became betrothed to 'Ā'isha, the daughter of Abū Bakr his oldest friend. All his efforts to win over members of other tribes were thwarted by the Meccans, until there came a handful of men from

Medina who were to change the course of the world's history. It is sobering to reflect how the most momentous results may follow from most insignificant happenings. Had these men not come to the pilgrimage festival that year, had the Quraysh not been over-confident that Muhammad's preaching would be ineffective and so made little or no attempt to interfere with him at this moment, the lives of millions would not have been fundamentally changed. These six pilgrims listened to the prophet's message, accepted Islam, and went back to Medina as missionaries on his behalf. The times were propitious: Medina had been unsettled by wars and murders caused by the rivalry of the two tribes Aus and Khazraj, the first supported by the Jews of the Banū Qurayza and al-Nadīr, the second backed by the Qainuqā' Jews. Both parties were weary of strife. Muhammad arranged to meet the Medinans in the following year at Minā; and this time a dozen came and accepted Islam at 'Aqaba, so named from a small hill at the place. On their return these men were extraordinarily successful in converting their fellow-townsmen to Islam. It seems to have been the fate of Judaism to attract men of every nation under heaven by its sublime truth and yet to lose them for reasons which need not concern us here. Muhammad followed the path taken by Christian preaching six centuries earlier when he addressed his message to those who had been prepared for monotheism by Jewish teaching. Indeed, he went further: by denying the divinity of Jesus he brought peace to Arabian Christian lands which had suffered bitterly from Christological disputes. But the price was the unconditional surrender of the essence of Christianity.

The Muhammadan era had dawned. The following year, 622, seventy-five pilgrims pledged their support. They would defend the prophet against all comers. These happenings could not be concealed from the Quraysh, who pursued the returning pilgrims, but though they managed to seize one or two they could not prevent the main body from regaining their native town. Thoroughly aroused, they began to oppress the Muslims with such severity that Muhammad decided to order his followers to migrate to Medina, and more than a hundred slipped away, until Abū Bakr and 'Alī were the only ones to stay behind voluntarily. Muhammad left the latter behind to look after the women and children, and taking what money they had he and Abū Bakr withdrew by night to a cave on Mount Thaur. This was a wise precaution, since it lay to the south of Mecca, whereas Medina was to the north-east and the Meccans would naturally pursue them in that direction. Here they stayed for some time, being provisioned by Abū Bakr's son, who brought them news of their enemies' movements. When the coast was clear they travelled by a devious route to Medina, where they received an enthusiastic welcome.

From the outset Muhammad displayed the tact and diplomacy which marked all his dealings with others. Beset by appeals from all sides to take up his abode with individuals who perforce belonged to one party and thus were disliked by the other, he instantly evolved a plan which would hurt the feelings of none and at the same time absolve him from the responsibility of an invidious choice. He left the choice to his camel. It came to rest in the quarter of the Najjār clan of the Khazraj who were, as we have seen, relations of his. 'Umar when he became Caliph gave expression to the feeling of all Muslims to this day that a new era began with the migration to Medina, though the actual date was not adopted, but New Year's day of the year in which it occurred, that is

July 15/16, A.D. 622. The word *hijra* does not mean 'flight', or even 'migration', so much as the breaking of old ties, and so marks the fact that Muhammad now belonged to Medina and not to Mecca, with all the consequences that were to follow.

Muhammad was no longer a persecuted citizen of Mecca, but the leader of a religious community acknowledged to possess divine authority. This change in his status can be seen in the tone of many of the Medinan sūras, which speak with the voice of authority not only in spiritual and ethical matters, but also in matters of everyday life.

From the first it was evident that Muhammad believed that his message was for all Arabs – and perhaps for all mankind – and it had now become clear that they could be made to listen only by force. There could be no compromise with idolatry. Therefore it followed that all those who refused to believe in Islam must be quelled. Idolaters whose very existence was an insult to the one true God would have to accept Islam or the sword; other monotheists would have to acknowledge their inferiority by paying a special tax. This became the established principle of Islam during the few years of the prophet's life at Medina which remained after the opposition of the Quraysh was quelled. It was put into effect in the whole of the Arab empire in the century that followed.

Muhammad's first task was to build up a self-contained community which would hold together and maintain its position despite the force of tradition and a long history of rivalries and feuds. To do this successfully required consummate ability, diplomacy, firmness, and far-sightedness. A certain amount of resentment at his assumption of authority was shown by the leading Medinans, who not unnaturally felt that they had given up more than they had gained; there were the rival claims of the Muslims of Medina, called 'the helpers', on the one hand, and the refugees from Mecca on the other; and last, but not least, there were the powerful Jewish clans and tribes who soon showed their dislike of Muhammad's religion and his policy.

An abstract from a charter which Muhammad drew up, probably a year or two after his arrival in Medina, shows how the brotherhood of Islam took precedence of all other ties and relationships, so that a believing father might have to slay an unbelieving son. This brotherhood bound all Muslims together for offence and defence, guaranteed them the protection of the community, except when a man was an obvious offender, and made God and his prophet the final arbiter in all disputes. Various Jewish tribes are mentioned by name as sharing in this charter as 'a community along with the Muslims', while retaining their own religion. They were guaranteed the same privileges and were under the same financial and other obligations as the Muslims.

So far so good. But a religious movement must move; it cannot survive without progress and expansion. Signs are not wanting that there was considerable economic stress in Medina, and action was called for if the enthusiasm of the tiny community was not to dissipate. From the beginning Muhammad had dedicated himself to the task of converting the Arabs to Islam, particularly those of his own town and kin. Above all, he desired to see the Ka'ba purified and given to Allāh. Peaceful efforts had been ineffective and the time for forceful action had come.

Muhammad accomplished his purpose in the course of three small engagements: the number of combatants in these never exceeded a few thousand, but in importance they rank among the world's decisive battles. The systematic destruction of the Jewish communities, both a political and a religious necessity, was a mere interlude in his victorious progress in the Hijāz. The first step was the most difficult, for it was no easy matter to persuade the Medinans to attack their old friends in Mecca, with whom they were linked by marriage, commerce, and the ancient pilgrim rites. And the Meccan emigrants, too, must be persuaded to take up arms against, and in the last resort to kill, their heathen kinsmen. Blood relationship, it will be remembered, was a sacred tie recognized by all Arabs and sanctioned by usage as old as the people itself. However, by the preaching of war as a sacred duty (*jihād*) Muhammad gradually induced his followers to attack the Meccans. A beginning was made with what nowadays would be called a frontier incident. Mecca depended largely on its trade, which has been valued (perhaps overvalued) at more than 300,000 gold pounds per annum, from which the Meccans would claim a large percentage. A better centre than Medina for cutting the trade-route to Syria could not have been found. No more than ten men were concerned in the first successful raid: six Muslims attacked a caravan guarded by four Quraysh, killed one, and took two prisoners; one man got away. As this attack was made in the sacred month when war was banned throughout Arabia, something like dismay was felt in Medina when the emigrants turned up with the spoil. Muhammad had run counter to Arab feeling, and most European writers take an unfavourable view of his action. His own view or, as Muslims would say, God's judgement, is expressed in sūra 2:214: 'They will question you (O Muhammad) with regard to warfare in the sacred month; say: Warfare therein is a serious matter; but to turn (men) from the way of God and to disbelieve in Him and in the sacred temple and to drive his people from it is more serious with God, and infidelity is more serious than killing.' In other words, to break a truce by which all Arabs have hitherto been bound is no light matter, but scruples of this kind cannot be allowed to override the necessity of bringing idolatry to an end.

From this point events moved rapidly. A force of some three hundred Muslims led by the prophet himself attacked and routed about a thousand Meccans at Badr. Two factors were decisive in this victory: the spirit of religious fervour kindled in the hearts of the Muslims coupled with a strong faith in God's assistance, and the great skill of the prophet in choosing the terrain on which to fight. In this engagement some of his most determined opponents were slain, and many prisoners were taken to Medina to await ransom. Nothing succeeds like success, and the bedouin now began to attach themselves to the new movement in increasing numbers, and the cautious in Medina who preferred to sit on the fence as long as possible openly joined the prophet, while in Mecca rage and consternation seized the Quraysh. This fight figures largely in Muslim tradition and in the Qurān, and must be regarded as the foundation of all the subsequent successes of Muslim armies.

At this point Muhammad began a series of operations which was to end with the expulsion of the Jews from the Hijāz. They had irritated him by their refusal to recognize him as a prophet; by ridicule and by argument; and of course their economic supremacy referred to in the last chapter was a standing irritant. At his instigation one or two Jews were murdered and no blood-money was paid to their next-of-kin.

Muhammad's relations with the Jews had never been easy.

Their leaders opposed his claim to be an apostle sent by God, and though they doubtless drew some satisfaction from his acceptance of the divine mission of Abraham, Moses, and the prophets, they could hardly be expected to welcome the inclusion of Jesus and Ishmael among his chosen messengers. The earliest biographer states that when Muhammad recited the verse (3:78) which asserts his belief in Jesus as a prophet sent by God, the most prominent Jews of Medina said that they had no belief in Jesus nor in anyone who believed in him. About this time Muhammad, who had hitherto prayed with his face towards Jerusalem after the manner of the Jews, now faced about and prayed towards Mecca. He claimed Abraham and Ishmael as founders of the Ka'ba and of Arabian monotheism pure and undefiled, and thus independent of, and prior to, both Judaism and Christianity.

Doubtless, too, the existence of pockets of disaffected Jews in and around his base was a cause of uneasiness and they had to be eliminated if he was to wage war without anxiety. The first community to suffer was the Qainuqā' who were for the most part goldsmiths. They had supported the Aus, one of the rival Arab tribes in Medina, before the prophet's arrival, and to this fact they owed their lives; for when they were forced to surrender the prophet condemned them to death, but at the intercession of the leader of the Aus he gave them their lives, but compelled them to leave the country.

In the third year of the hijra a rich caravan fell into his hands and the Quraysh were determined to make an end of their enemy. They equipped a force of some 3000 men and marched on Medina. Muhammad wisely ordered his men to stay within the town and retain all the advantages of a strong position from which they could shoot at the enemy in the open; but his followers were so headstrong that against his better judgement he had to yield to their clamorous demand to go out and fight the enemy. The opposing forces met at Uhud, about a mile from the town. The Muslims, only 700 strong, were put to flight after an initial success, and Muhammad himself was wounded by a swordstroke which cost him two teeth. Why the Meccans did not pursue their victory and annihilate their opponents remains a mystery. A report circulated that Muhammad had been slain, but as the Meccan leader is reported to have heard 'Umar declare that the prophet was safe with him the Meccans cannot have thought that they had disposed of their rival. Perhaps it was the old Arab conception of war as a chivalrous defence of honour which saved the Muslims. Honour was satisfied when the shame of defeat was removed by victory, and no further effort was called for. Casualties in purely Arab campaigns have seldom been heavy, and this was an age when war was a pastime and a means of gaining loot, rather like some of the campaigns in medieval Europe. The Muslims lost seventy men killed.

Nothing will better illustrate Muhammad's spirit than his action in insisting on following up the enemy the following day. Despite his wounds and those of his supporters he marched out in the direction of Mecca, and when he encamped he ordered a large fire to be kindled so that the Quraysh were bound to notice his defiance. He stayed there for some days and then returned to the city. This masterly act could not fail to raise the morale of his men. He had to face a difficult situation. If Badr was a proof that God was on their side, what could be said of Uhud? Lamentation and woe were heard on all sides, and many who mourned the loss of a father or brother blamed Muhammad as the author of their calamity. His answer came in sūra 3:134 ff., which may be summarized thus:

If you have suffered a blow, so did the enemy at Badr, and wars come to provide martyrs and that God may prove those who believe. Paradise is only to be attained when God knows who will really strive and endure. You used to wish for death before you met it, and now you have seen what it is. Every man dies when God permits – it is all written down – and the best of this world and the next is only for those who are steadfast in the way of God. Don't think that the idolaters will ultimately triumph. Victory was in your hands until you disobeyed God's Apostle and the archers left their post to plunder the enemy's camp. You were put to flight because you sought worldly gain. God allowed you to be defeated in order to test you, and now He has forgiven you. If God helps you none can overcome you: if He abandons you who then can help you? So let the believers rely upon God.

Soon afterwards the Nadīr, a tribe of Jews in the neighbourhood of Medina, fell under suspicion of treachery and were forced to lay down their arms and evacuate their settlements. Valuable land and much booty fell into the hands of the Muslims. Muhammad had strengthened his position by a bloodless victory, and the lack of loyalty and cohesion among the Jews themselves had become fatally apparent. The neighbouring tribe of Qurayza who were soon to suffer annihilation made no move to help their co-religionists, and their allies, the Aus, were afraid to give them active support.

The last stage in Muhammad's triumphant advance was now at hand. The Meccans for the last time prepared an expedition against Medina. An exiled Jewish chief took a prominent part in enlisting the aid of bedouin tribes, and finally a force of some 10,000 men took the field. Great alarm was felt in Medina where the memory of Uhud was still fresh. Though Muhammad always reserved the right to make the final decision he showed his wisdom in consulting those about him. On this occasion he took the advice of a Persian convert and dug a deep ditch to cover the approach to the town where it lay open to attack so that the town could not be captured by a rapid assault unless the enemy were prepared to face heavy casualties. The Quraysh were disconcerted and withdrew to an encampment, shooting arrows at long range against the defenders. Meanwhile, both sides endeavoured to sow dissension in the ranks of their opponents. The Quraysh succeeded in detaching the Jewish tribe of Qurayza, but Muhammad cleverly countered this move by sending an emissary who made the Jews distrust the Meccans and induced the Meccans to distrust the Jews. Only one assault, and that a half-hearted one, was made, and the attackers were driven off. The killed on both sides amounted to eight only. Arabia is not a country in which long sieges can be undertaken without water and modern means of transport, and the besiegers began to suffer from hunger and bad weather. The Jews would not make their pro-mised diversionary attack for fear of being left in the lurch, so the bedouin withdrew and the Quraysh returned to Mecca.

Muhammad immediately turned on the Jews, who after a short siege surrendered unconditionally. Their old allies the Aus pleaded for them, and Muhammad asked them whether they would accept the judgement of one of their own chiefs. They agreed, and thereupon he appointed a man who was suffering from a deadly wound, whose verdict was that the men should be put to death and the women and children sold as slaves. The sentence was carried out; the prisoners were led out in batches, beheaded on the edge of a trench which had been dug in the market-place, and thrown in. The execution of some 800 men occupied the whole day and went on far into the night. Only one Jew abjured his religion to save his life. The rest, after prayer and reading of the scriptures, went calmly to their death. This mass execution has excited bitter comment from most Orientalists. But it ought to be borne in mind that our generation has learned to its dismay that there are nations who believe that 'total war', involving even the death of women and children, is justifiable if it crushes the enemy's will to fight and saves further bloodshed; and further, no man with a weapon in his hand need surrender. Nominal Christians and Jews have done similar and worse things in the cause of national, religious, or social security, and the fault lies not in religion but in sinful human nature. However, one does not expect such acts from one who comes with a message from the Compassionate and Merciful.

Muhammad now began a systematic encirclement of Mecca by subduing the neighbouring tribes. That accomplished, he set forth with a strong detachment to attend the pilgrimage in A.H. 6. The Meccans bitterly resented his intrusion and refused to permit him to enter the sacred territory that year: but Muhammad gained a great diplomatic victory in a treaty which was drawn up at Hudaybiya. In this the Quraysh recognized his right to proselytize without hindrance and agreed to allow him and his followers to visit Mecca the following year in exchange for a ten years' truce. By this armistice with the Meccans he removed the obstacle which prevented the bedouin from joining the Muslims, and from now on the Arabs flocked to Muhammad in hundreds.

The prophet was to live but four more years; during this short time the shape of the Near East was settled for centuries

to come. Khaybar, one of the last remaining Jewish strongholds, was attacked suddenly; and though the inhabitants
fought more bravely here than elsewhere, outnumbered and
caught off their guard, they were defeated. After stipulating
that their lives should be spared they surrendered with all
their possessions. Their chief had hidden his precious metals,
but another Jew betrayed his secret and fetched some of them,
and the Muslims tortured the unfortunate chief to extract
information about the remainder. He and his cousin were the
only Jews to be put to death at Khaybar, with one important
exception – the Jewess Zaynab, who may have been the cause
of the prophet's subsequent death. She had lost all her men-
folk in the battle, and invited Muhammad, Abū Bakr, and
others to dine off a lamb which she had poisoned. After
swallowing one mouthful, the prophet spat out the rest, cry-
ing that the meat had been poisoned. He was seized with
violent cramp and pain, and complained of the effect of the
poison to his dying day. One of his companions died of the
poison, and of course Zaynab was put to death.

The capture of Khaybar had an importance of its own, for
it laid down a principle which with some modification was
adopted by the Muslims when they occupied the vast territories of the exhausted empires of Byzantium and Persia. The
Jews were allowed to keep their land on condition that they
surrendered half the produce to Medina. However, the
arrangement did not last long, for 'Umar, always sterner
than his master, expatriated the Jews with all the other Jews
and Christians in the peninsula.

The Jewish colonies at other centres surrendered on the
same terms without offering resistance. Much of the wealth
of the country which had been concentrated in the hands of
the Jews had now been seized by the Muslims, who were no

longer indigent immigrants but wealthy landowners, men of substance, owning camels and horses and their own weapons – always costly possessions in Arabia. Muhammad's fame spread far and wide, and the bedouin flocked to him in thousands.

In the following year Muhammad entered Mecca as a pilgrim accompanied by a large force of devoted followers. The Meccans, faithful to their agreement, withdrew to the hills, where they saw the man they had ejected enter in triumph. Muhammad went round the Ka'ba seven times, and touched the black stone with his staff. This done, sacrifices were offered at Marwa, and the following day the prophet's muezzin mounted the roof of the Ka'ba and called the Muslims to prayer. The agreement of Hudaybiya allowed him only a three-day sojourn in Mecca, and Muhammad, who had married another wife, wanted to stay on; but the Meccans refused to allow the wedding feast to take place after the time stipulated had elapsed, and on the fourth night he set out for Medina. During this short visit to Mecca he won over the famous general Khālid and two other prominent men. The tide had turned, and signs were not wanting that the Quraysh were sick of strife; and now that the position of Mecca as a centre of pilgrimage was safe for all time, all heart had gone out of the struggle. In A.H. 8 (A.D. 630) the Quraysh were foolish enough to attack a tribe under Muslim protection, and so the truce was broken. At the head of some 10,000 men Muhammad marched on Mecca. Abū Sufyān, who had been the prophet's most redoubtable opponent, made his peace with Muhammad and accepted Islam. He returned to the city with the promise that none who kept within doors should be injured. Some slight opposition was encountered, and the defenders were annihilated by Khālid, who incurred the prophet's anger by his excessive zeal. Muhammad entered as a conqueror. Immediately he destroyed the images of the gods, demanded the key of the temple, and entered to pray. He returned the key to its hereditary custodian and confirmed others in their old offices. The sacred territory was carefully delimited and the Ka'ba was established as the centre of Islam. In the hour of victory Muhammad showed his magnanimity: only four people were put to death. Three according to the laws of war deserved their fate; the fourth was a singing girl who had composed satirical verses against the prophet. The prophet's clemency was rewarded: the whole city accepted him as the apostle of God, and within a few weeks a large force of Meccans was fighting side by side with his tried companions and helpers. Indeed so generous was he to the Meccans when dividing the spoil of later raids that the Medinans complained that they were being unfairly treated. Muhammad replied that though they had helped him in his need he, too, by God's assistance had brought them internal peace and rich material reward, and for his part he was resolved never to leave them whatever happened. Deeply moved, they withdrew their words. However, the Qurān (sūra 9:58 f.) lays down the principle that among the objects of almsgiving is the 'gaining of men's hearts'. Islam, which like Christianity began as the religion of a despised minority, had now become the religion of the State, and it was to everyone's interest to conform to it. Poets who once satirized and ridiculed Muhammad vied one with another in laudatory verse; bedouin chiefs submitted and offered their men for his raids. Far-away Bahrayn paid taxes and the nearer tribes the tithe.

At this time Muhammad modified his attitude towards the Christians. It must be remembered that Christian Arabs are always indicated. Many of these were unwilling as yet to accept Islam. Sūra 9:29 f. reads:

Fight those who do not believe in Allah, and the Last Day, and do not forbid what God and his apostle have forbidden, and do not follow the true religion of those to whom scriptures were given, until they pay tribute out of hand, being brought low. The Jews say Ezra is the son of God, while the Christians say Christ is the son of God. That is what they say with their mouths, imitating the speech of those who disbelieved aforetime. May God fight them, how perverse they are! They choose their rabbis and monks as lords instead of God and the Messiah the son of Mary. But they were ordered to worship one God alone. There is no God but He. He is far above what they associate with Him. . . . He it is who has sent His apostle with guidance and true religion to make it triumphant over every religion, however much the 'associators' may dislike the fact. O believers, many rabbis and monks devour man's wealth wantonly and debar men from the way of God. And those who hoard gold and silver without spending it in God's way, tell them, O prophet, of a painful punishment.

Muslim lawyers differ as to the meaning of these categories: it is possible that they refer only to those Jews and Christians who are not faithful to their scriptures. No doubt complaints of the tyranny of monks towards other Christian sects would be common, and undoubtedly some monastic institutions were wealthy. The charge against the Jews of worshipping Ezra has always remained a mystery; monotheism is of course the centre of the Jewish creed. The sad result of this passage is that it authorizes application of the odious term *mushrik* to Jews and Christians. Up to this time it could only be applied to the heathen who by worshipping Allāh's daughters associated other gods with him, and so *mushrik* properly means polytheist. More will be said on this subject later: here it need only be pointed out that the term 'Mother of God' given to the Virgin Mary could mean only one thing to an Arab – the sexual trinity of the old heathen world, which was never a unity.

Muhammad's armies were now reaching out to areas occupied by Christian or Christianized Arabs, and it was necessary to define their relation to Muslims: they must pay tribute or take the consequences. One of Muhammad's last expeditions was directed against the Byzantines. The Muslims got as far as Tabūk, and then for reasons unknown withdrew, having achieved little more than the submission of the Christian John of Ayla, a small port on the Gulf of 'Aqaba. Muhammad guaranteed the safety and property of the community on payment of an annual tribute, and left his agents there to collect it. This treaty was honoured for more than a century. One or two small settlements on the other side of the gulf were similarly treated.

Muhammad went on pilgrimage for the last time, and after his return to Medina arranged for an expedition to the Syrian frontier; on the following day he fell into a fever and lay sick for several days. He got up to attend prayers at the mosque, but the effort was too great, and he died the same day.

The foregoing is a brief objective account of Muhammad's life drawn from his biography. The facts have been left to speak for themselves. Trustworthy tradition depicts a man of amazing ability in winning men's hearts by persuasion and in coercing and disarming his opponents. If we ignore the legendary claims to miraculous powers – powers which he himself expressly disclaimed – he stands out as one of the great figures of history. (Here it is right to point out that generally the hagiological legends have no historical backing: no names guarantee their authenticity, and the biographer doubtless wishes us to understand that they are stories repeated by the pious and credulous.) Far more worthy of credence are those stories which go far to explain, when taken with his generosity and kindness, why men loved him. 'Umar, whose severity and violence were feared by all, once visited the prophet when his womenfolk were talking loudly and excitedly in his presence. When 'Umar entered they ran incontinently behind the curtain. 'Umar angrily wanted to know why they should show him more respect than the prophet. The latter, who had evidently enjoyed the innocent chatter of the women, said: 'Umar, if the devil himself were to meet you in the street he would dodge into a side alley!'

A woman barely escaped with her life from some raiders by galloping off on one of the prophet's own camels. After recounting the story of the raid she said: 'I vowed to sacrifice the camel to God if he saved me by her.' The prophet smiled and replied: 'That's a poor reward! God saved you by her, and then you want to kill her! Leave the animal alone, for anyhow it is my property; and go home with God's blessing.'

From the books of tradition we learn that the prophet was subject to ecstatic seizures. He is reported to have said that when inspiration came to him he felt as it were the painful sounding of a bell. Even in cold weather his forehead was bathed in sweat. On one occasion he called to his wife to wrap him in a veil. At other times visions came to him in sleep. Religious ecstasy is a world-wide phenomenon in one stage of human society, and in its early stages Muhammad's verses were couched in the Semitic form of mantic oracular utterance. The veiling of the head and the use of rhymed prose were marks of the Arabian soothsayer, while the feeling of physical violence and compulsion, and the outward appearance of 'possession' which seemed to the onlookers to indicate madness of demonic possession were sometimes recorded by, or observed in, the Hebrew prophets.

The Qurān as we have it now is a record of what Muhammad said while in the state or states just mentioned. It is beyond doubt that his hearers recognized the symptoms of revelation, otherwise his *obiter dicta* which the literature of tradition purports to record would be included in the Qurān.

There is no doubt that at the death of Muhammad a good deal of the Qurān was already written down, though not all of it, for while he was alive new suras or chapters were constantly being added. One of the secretaries he employed boasted that he had induced the prophet to alter the wording of the revelations. Nor is there any doubt that a great deal of the Qurān had been learned by heart, for professional remembrancers who could repeat the whole of a poet's compositions had long been recognized as indispensable members of Arabian society, so that there was available a goodly supply of men with memories prodigious by our standards. In one passage of the Qurān it seems to be implied that

Muhammad could not read till late in life (though it is possible that the statement refers to the Jewish and Christian scriptures) and it definitely states that he did not himself write down the Qurān; but someone else must have done, for the passage goes on to say that the Qurān is read to the Meccans. The latter had accused the prophet of writing down old fables and stories told him by foreigners. However, an early tradition says that he himself wrote on the day that the treaty was made at Hudaybiya, and it is not at all likely that the prophet was content to rely on his associates to read a letter or, in his early days, a bill of lading. It is a poor compliment to call him 'the illiterate prophet' as some of his followers do.

The recording of the prophet's words in the beginning was haphazard. Verses were written on palm leaves, stones, the shoulder-blades of animals – in short, on any material which was available. Tradition associates the collection of all this material, together with what men had committed to memory, to Abū Bakr, the first Caliph, and alternatively to his successor 'Umar who died before the work was completed. The prophet's secretary Zayd is said to have given all that he had collected to Abū Bakr, written out on separate leaves. The latter bequeathed these to 'Umar's daughter Hafsa, one of the prophet's widows. Before an authorized version was established under the caliph 'Uthmān there were four rival editions in use. These have long since disappeared, but we are told that they differed from the authorized version, some containing more and some less than the latter. When men who had learned one version came into conflict with those who possessed a rival version it was feared that scriptural exegesis would pursue the course it had taken among Jews and Christians who at that time accused the one the other of corrupting and falsifying the sacred text. 'Uthmān then entrusted a commission, in which Zayd took a prominent place, with the task of preparing a text which everyone must accept. Only the men of Kūfa refused the new edition, and their version was certainly extant as late as A.D. 1000. 'Uthmān's edition to this day remains the authoritative word of God to Muslims. Nevertheless, even now variant readings, involving not only a different reading of the vowels but also occasionally a different consonantal text, are recognized as of equal authority one with another. The old Kufic script in which the Qurān was originally written contained no indication of vowels, and so the consonants of verbs could be read as actives or passives, and, worse still, many of the consonants themselves could not be distinguished without the diacritical dots which were afterwards added, when and by whom we do not know.

Thus it will be seen that the textual history of the Qurān is very similar to that of the Bible. Originally considerable freedom prevailed, until a later generation insisted on uniformity but never entirely achieved it. The parallel goes further. The arrangement of the text is arbitrary and haphazard. Just as in the prophetical books of the Old Testament there is seldom any indication of the occasion on which the words were spoken, and scholars have to reconstruct the background, removing whole passages from their context to fit them into a chronological scheme and a historical situation to which they may or may not belong, so in the Qurān, which is arranged on the purely mechanical plan of putting the longest chapters first and the shortest last, scholars, eastern and western alike, have been busy for centuries in trying to determine to what period of the prophet's ministry a particular sūra belongs. The problem is further complicated

by the inclusion of verses which must have been spoken at
Medina in sūras which begin in Mecca.

Nevertheless, in spite of what has been said above on the
authority of early Arab writers, it must always be remembered that to Muslims the Qurān is a faithful and unalterable
reproduction of the original scriptures which are preserved
in heaven, and this in spite of the fact that the Qurān teaches,
and almost everyone holds, that a large number of verses are
superseded and abrogated by later revelations.[1] The Muslim
world has not yet come to grips with the problem which
Christian Europe faced after the Renaissance, but signs are
not wanting that thoughtful Muslims are seeking a way out
of the logical impasse.

Muslim tradition is all but unanimous that the beginning
of sūra 96 contains Muhammad's call to rise as a prophet.
'Recite thou in the name of thy Lord', etc. 'Recite' might
mean 'read', for until comparatively modern times men
moved their lips and formed the words they read, because it
was difficult or impossible for them to grasp the meaning of
a document without uttering its words. Thus here we have
at least an adumbration of the theory that the Qurān is a copy
or transcription of the tablet preserved in heaven, an idea
which goes back thousands of years to the early Sumerians,
to reappear in Jewish and Muslim belief. Heaven was a place
inhabited by God and his angels. He had his throne and
attendants with books and records, and Muslims believe that
on the resurrection day they will gaze upon Him.

As has been said, it is impossible to feel sure ground beneath one in arranging the contents of the Qurān in a strictly
chronological order, and any reconstruction apart from un-
disputed sūras of early Meccan origin must depend on

1. This subject is discussed in the final chapter.

subjective criticism. Until all the rival readings scattered in manuscripts and books not readily to be consulted have been collected on a scale comparable with the critical apparatus of the Bible, and until a trustworthy lexicon of the Qurān has been compiled, details – many of great importance – will remain obscure, and the following account of the internal development of the Qurān can only proceed on a broad front wherein lie many 'pockets' that resist analysis. The early sūras are marked by rhyme and by conjurations of nature: 'by the moon', 'by the morn', 'by the heavens', and so on. The dominating note is the warning of hell awaiting idolaters, the unjust, and the selfish rich. God is the sole creator of the universe, and he who gave life will renew man's life after death when the body will rise from the grave. Paradise, a garden intersected by rivers and filled with luscious fruits, awaits believers; there they will be waited on by dark-eyed houris and beautiful youths and drink wine from golden bowls. The luxurious delights of Paradise are described again and again in liveliest colour over against the tortures of hell in black smoke and awful heat in which the wicked fill their bellies with boiling water. God will forgive men's lesser crimes, but major sins will meet with terrible retribution, so let none feel safe from the chastisement to come.

Later Muhammad claimed to come with a message from God which confirmed the writings which had been revealed to Jews and Christians, and we naturally postulate some intercourse between him and them. It seems natural to suppose that in his search for God, disappointed and disgusted as he was with the heathenism of Mecca, he was originally awakened to the existence of the God of Jews and Christians, and when he appeared openly as a prophet he looked to them for support. As a member of a heathen family preaching monotheism he would naturally be drawn toward them. At any rate the purely Arabian character of his preaching became gradually intermixed with references to revered figures of the Old Testament, and later to Jesus and his apostles. And this raises a very interesting point. What possible interest would the Meccans have in 'the books of Abraham and Moses'; and what did they know about Noah and the Ark and Pharaoh; of the angels' visit to Abraham and the promise to him of a son in his old age? These and the many references to the Old Testament surely imply either a Jewish audience or a circle acquainted with the broad outlines of the Old Testament stories.

As Muhammad's preaching develops, more and more is borrowed from this source, until in the sūra called *Joseph* he shows that he is acquainted not only with the account of the patriarch's career as it is set forth in the book of Genesis, but also with the later Jewish development of the story. As we have seen, Jewish opposition in Medina became a serious hindrance to his prestige. The Jews ridiculed him and refused to answer questions. But by this time Muhammad had learned that Abraham preceded Moses and Jesus and that he was the father of Ishmael and was thus the ancestor of the Arabs. Abraham and Ishmael he associates with the building of the Ka'ba. Abraham, he claims, was a Muslim, and thus at a stroke the primitive and apostolic character of Islam was established. But there is no historical evidence for the assertion that Abraham or Ishmael was ever in Mecca, and if there had been such a tradition it would have to be explained how all memory of the old Semitic name Ishmael (which was known in its true Arabian form in Arabian inscriptions and written correctly with an initial consonant Y) came to be lost. The form in the Qurān is taken either from Greek or

Syriac sources. Isaac and Israel are further examples of such borrowings, and the forms Yūnus, and Ilyās (Jonah and Elijah) are patently Greek. If any of these worthies had been familiar to Muhammad's hearers it is inconceivable that their names would have been recited to them in a Greek or Aramaic form: alternatively if they did know these names they must have heard of them from Jews or Christians. Therefore when the Meccans accused him of composing the Qurān with the help of strangers who dictated ancient tales to him by night and day there was some justification for the charge when we find clear philological proof, apart from Talmudic legends like that of Satan's refusal to worship Adam, of the foreign origin of what claims to be an Arabian Qurān. The ordinary reader can hardly be expected to plunge into the intricacies of comparative Semitic philology, and therefore the proof of the statement that many words in the Qurān cannot be explained from Arabic and must be traced back to their source in Hebrew or Syriac before they can be made to yield a meaning must be sought elsewhere. But the point is most important, especially as the Qurān claims to be an Arabic Qurān and a revelation to the Arabs in plain unequivocal language. Anyone who cares to consult an Arabic commentary on the Qurān will see that there were very many words which the commentators could not understand. However it does not follow that they were unintelligible to Muhammad's hearers, many of whom were familair with Jews and Christians, and cannot but have enlarged their vocabulary in the course of their journeys in the caravans of Quraysh which went forth from Mecca in all directions to the Byzantine, Persian, and Yaman borders. The latter would probably account for the presence of Abyssinian words in the Qurān.

THE TEACHING OF THE QURĀN

Next to the doctrine of the absolute oneness of God, perhaps the most important assertion in the Qurān is that God has revealed his will to men through apostles who brought a written message; and the Qurān, last in time and the completion of all that had gone before, was in strict agreement with the earlier scriptures and explained, and where necessary modified or abrogated, part of their teaching. 'Believe in God and His Apostle and the book which He has sent down to His Apostle and the book which He sent down formerly. He who disbelieves in God and His angels, His books, and His apostles, and the Last Day, has strayed far [from the truth].' (Sūra 4:135.)

Muhammad held firmly to the belief that God had revealed his will to Jews and Christians, but they could not agree either to follow God's commands or to live at unity among themselves. If Jews held Christians to be blasphemous innovators and Christians called Jews unbelievers and persecuted their own co-religionists for holding divergent views about the nature of Jesus, they must either have corrupted the original scriptures or followed their own mischievous imaginations. They must be brought back to first principles – to the original truth taught by Abraham. This was Islam, a word which, contrary to analogy, appears to mean submission or resignation to God. It is therefore a term which in its widest sense could be used by all monotheists, and I have myself claimed to be a Muslim in the proper sense of the word, in accordance with sūra 28:53, which states that the people of the scriptures say: 'Verily before it [i.e. the Qurān] we were self-surrenderers' (Muslims); and sūra 3:45, where the disciples say to Jesus: 'We are God's helpers, we believe in God, so bear witness that we are Muslims.' (Incidentally this text is important in showing that the term 'Nazarene' had nothing to do with Nazareth in the Arab mind, but meant to Muhammad a God-helper, from the verb *nasara*, to aid. Nevertheless the term is one of reproach, and it is wise in Arabian countries to adopt the word *masīhī*, which means 'Christian'.) Still, in view of these two passages, it is strange to find that in sūra 6:163 the prophet says: 'I am the first of those who surrender [to him].'

It is impossible in this book to give a full account of the teaching of the Qurān. We have seen how the prophet persisted in the face of heavy odds in preaching the doctrine of one true God, and the Qurān shows us what his conception of God was. The formula 'compassionate and merciful' is familiar to almost everyone, and though the sufferings of the damned are painted in sombre colours, divine mercy and forgiveness are strongly emphasized. God's power is infinite, as is his knowledge. Though transcendent and above all similitude, he is nearer to man than the vein of his neck. Again, though not bound by man's ideas of justice and equity, God hates injustice and oppression, and requires kindness to orphans and widows and charity to the poor. The Muslim is not to fear death, for it is the gate of Paradise: patience and trust are incumbent on him. He must endure with fortitude the troubles and trials of life, and must put his trust in God at all times. This in the briefest possible terms is the moral basis of Islam, and only the prejudiced can deny that it has produced, and still produces, men of the highest character and integrity. Of course, like other religions, it has failed to keep men true to their obligations, and to some extent we must hold the theologians of the following centuries responsible for the laxness of society, and especially those who invented doctrines which they put into the mouth of the prophet and so got his authority for deeds and words which he would almost certainly have repudiated.

Before leaving this subject a passage (sūra 24:35 f.) which has given rise to one of the most famous mystical treatises in Islam deserves to be quoted. Not even its context – it is preceded by verses which deal with the accusation of immodesty or worse made against the prophet's favourite wife, and is followed by other mundane matter – can detract from its beauty and its testimony to the source of the prophet's convictions. 'God is the light of heaven and earth. His light may be compared to a niche which contains a lamp, the lamp within glass, and the glass as it were a star of pearl. It is lit from a blessed olive tree neither eastern nor western. Its oil would almost shine forth if no fire touched it. Light upon Light; God guideth to His Light whom He will.' This sūra goes on to describe the utter darkness and desolation of those who disbelieve in God, and returns lyrically to the thought of God praised by all creation, the birds in their flight, the fishes of the sea, and the beasts of the earth. The lightning's flash and the storm of hail and the procession of the life-bringing clouds are manifestations of his power and beneficence, and his majesty in nature.

The qurānic conception of angels is so far similar to the biblical conception as to need no comment; but it tells of a class of beings intermediate between men and angels with which we are unfamiliar. These are the *jinn*, who are created of fire. There are good and bad *jinn*. Some were very useful to Solomon in giving him occult knowledge: others are sometimes called satans. Their leader is 'the Satan' or Iblīs (a form of the Greek *diabolos* or devil).

In the matter of the Judgement Day the qurānic teaching

is similar to Jewish and Christian belief. None knows the hour but God; a trumpet will sound and the graves will give up their dead and all will be judged, their deeds be weighed in the balance, and – a new note – all will be given their account-book. If it is put into their right hand heaven will be their portion: if in the left they are doomed to hell.

Prayer. The most important of the ritual and moral duties incumbent on all Muslims are prayer, almsgiving, fasting, and pilgrimage. Custom and tradition have supplied the gaps which the Qurān leaves, and have welded its prescriptions into a well-defined system, based theoretically on the practice of the prophet himself. For the broad outlines doubtless the prophet's example was faithfully recorded and adopted; but for many of the details we have to thank the jurists who imposed their will on the community after much dissension. A full description of Muslim prayer with drawings to illustrate the various postures of the body will be found in Lane's *Manners and Customs of the Modern Egyptians*, one of the most instructive and thorough studies of a country's social, economic, and religious life which has ever been written. The Qurān appears to require only three prayers a day, but tradition insists upon five; the first begins at sunset, and is followed by the night, dawn, noon, and afternoon prayers. The faithful are called to prayer by the *muezzin*, who mounts a minaret of the mosque and from a circular gallery cries with a powerful and penetrating voice: 'God is most great. I testify that there is no God but Allāh. I testify that Muhammad is God's Apostle. Come to prayer, come to security. God is most great.' Each clause is repeated at least once, and the morning call reminds Muslims that 'prayer is better than sleep'. Any serious-minded European who understands these words as they are thus proclaimed cannot but be

impressed by the entreaty, so much more personal and evo-
cative than the ringing of a bell.

In every mosque there is a semi-circular recess called the
mihrāb, which the worshipper must face, because he is then
facing Mecca. He stands and says inaudibly that he intends to
recite so many *rak'as* or bowings. Then opening his hands
and touching the lobes of his ears with his thumbs he says
'Allahu Akbar', and then proceeds to recite the prayers that
go with the bowings. Lowering his hands and folding them,
the left hand within the right, he recites the *Fātiha*, the first
chapter of the Qurān. Omitting the formula which is pre-
faced to every chapter but the ninth of the Qurān this runs:

> Praise belongs to God, Lord of the Worlds,
> The Compassionate, the Merciful,
> King of the Day of Judgement,
> 'Tis Thee we worship and Thee we ask for help.
> Guide us on the straight path,
> The path of those whom Thou hast favoured,
> Not the path of those who incur Thine anger nor of those
>   who go astray.

A few other verses follow, often sūra 112: 'Say, God is One,
the eternal God; begetting not and unbegotten; none is equal
to Him.' He then bows from the hips with hands on knees,
saying, '[I extol] the perfection of my Lord the Great',
assumes an upright position with the words 'Allāhu Akbar'
(which are used at most stages), then, sinking gently to his
knees, he places his hands on the ground and his nose and face
also to the ground. During this prostration he uses the same
words as before. He then rises to his knees, sitting on his heels,
and performs a second prostration, using the same words.
The prayers of one *rak'a* are then completed. At the end of
the last *rak'a* he pronounces the credo, then looking over his

right shoulder he says, 'Peace be on you and the mercy of God', and then says the same words over his left shoulder.[1] In mosques and in all large gatherings complete uniformity is attained by appointing a leader called the *Imām*, who stands in front of the congregation facing the *mihrāb*, or, if prayer is performed out of doors, the direction of Mecca.

In general pattern a mosque (the word means 'place of prostration') is very similar to a church: a *mihrāb* takes the place of the altar; to the right is the pulpit with a flight of stairs; opposite is the lectern on which the Qurān stands. A mosque must have a court and one or more fountains for ablutions, for washing before prayer is obligatory and is very similar to Jewish practice. From my own observation I am able to verify Lane's words on Muslim worship today: 'The utmost solemnity and decorum are observed in the public worship of the Muslims. Their looks and behaviour in the mosque are not those of enthusiastic devotion but of calm and modest piety . . . they appear wholly absorbed in the adoration of their creator; humble and downcast, yet without affected humility, or a forced expression of humility.' The reader will have observed that apart from the testimony to Muhammad being the apostle of God there is nothing in the official worship of Islam in which a Christian could not join, and one who understands the words of praise and adoration is tempted to do so. A Christian who, like the writer, goes from a visit to the Church of the Holy Sepulchre with its warring, noisy, competitive sects to the peace and devotion of the Great Mosque of Jerusalem cannot but be saddened and chastened to find in the one what he was looking for in the other.

1. The exact posture to be assumed and the precise words to be used at each stage are given in Lane's book cited above.

In the prophet's time women attended public prayers in the mosques, standing behind the men, but there is a tradition that he said that it was better for them to pray at home, and so far as I am aware they do not attend public prayers. As has already been said, prostration in prayer is not, as is often supposed, a Muslim institution. It is essentially eastern, marking the suppliant's attitude towards his ruler or king, and so has passed naturally to all the eastern religions. Obviously European dress is utterly unfitted to Oriental posture in prayer.

Almsgiving. Alms are of two kinds: (*a*) obligatory, (*b*) voluntary. The first at once suggests the now all but defunct tithe, and in Muslim canon law is put at one-fortieth of a man's income in money or kind. In early days it was collected by civil servants. However, the two are not always clearly distinguished. The terms used, *zakāt* and *sadaqāt*, are borrowed from the Jewish law. The duty of almsgiving is now left to the conscience of the Muslim. In Great Britain humane laws now place the responsibility for the unemployed, sick, and aged on the community, and the professional beggar who haunts the towns of the East is no more with us.

Fasting. The Qurān expressly founds this rule on the practice of Jews and Christians, and orders that the fast continue throughout the month of Ramadān, the month in which the Qurān was revealed. This fast can be a very severe strain, because unlike the Jewish and Christian months, which fall at a definite period of the solar year, the months of the Muslim year, which is lunar, may begin at any season over a given period of years. During the fast no one may eat, drink, or smoke between sunrise and sunset, and when the temperature is over a hundred degrees in the shade to be deprived of water is a serious trial. Sick people and travellers are exempt, but are expected to fast an equal number of days when they are in a position to do so.

Pilgrimage (*hajj*). As we have seen, Mecca was a centre of pilgrimage long before Islam, how long none can say. The inference from the Qurān, sūra 22:25 f., is that Abraham initiated pilgrimage there. Sūra 2:192 f. commands Muslims to perform the pilgrimage and provides a 'ransom' of fasting, alms, or an offering. This passage presupposes the pilgrim rites: it does not explain them or set them out, for the obvious reason that those to whom it was addressed were perfectly familiar with them. We know that Muhammad suppressed certain customs and modified others; but unfortunately we do not know what the ceremony performed by the heathen Arabs actually was. A full account will be found in Burton's *Pilgrimage*, and since his day many others have described the ritual. The *hajj* strictly is not completed without a visit to the prophet's tomb at Medina, and every Muslim ought to make the journey once in a lifetime. The pilgrims circumambulate the Ka'ba seven times, then run between the two small hills of Safā and Marwa hard by, and gather together at the hill of 'Arafāt twelve miles away; on the way back they sacrifice sheep and camels at Minā, where the ceremonial stoning of the devil takes place. One of the most important acts in the pilgrim ceremonial is the kissing of the black stone set in a wall of the Ka'ba. The original ritual required the pilgrims to be nude, but Muhammad ordered that when the pilgrim came within the sacred territory he was to lay aside his ordinary clothes and put on two plain sheets, leaving the face and head bare. Thenceforward a state of taboo exists: he must not cut his hair or pare his nails or have sexual intercourse until after the sacrifice at Minā.

To these four binding duties is added the profession of faith in Allāh and his apostle, and the five 'Pillars of the Faith' are complete.

As everyone knows, wine and pork are taboo to the Muslim, and idolatry is an unforgivable sin. There is no formal parallel to the Ten Commandments in the Qurān, but sūra 17:23–40 contains in other words the first, fifth, sixth, seventh, eighth, ninth, and tenth. Ostentatious waste, pride, and haughtiness are condemned, and the faithful are ordered to give just weight and measure. Slavery is a recognized institution, but slaves must be kindly treated, allowed to marry, and encouraged to buy their liberty. Better still if the master frees a believing slave. Women slaves may be used as concubines, but their owner must not make money by pandering; if he does not want them himself he must arrange for their marriage.

The Qurān has more to say on the position of women than on any other social question. The guiding note is sounded in the words, 'Women are your tillage', and the word for marriage is that used for the sexual act. The primary object of marriage is the propagation of children, and partly for this and partly for other reasons a man is allowed four wives at a time and an unlimited number of concubines. However, it is laid down that wives are to be treated with kindness and strict impartiality; if a man cannot treat all alike he should keep to one. The husband pays the woman a dowry at the time of marriage, and the money or property so allotted remains her own. The husband may divorce his wife at any time, but he cannot take her back until she has remarried and been divorced by a second husband. A woman cannot sue for divorce on any grounds, and her husband may beat her. In this matter of the status of women lies the greatest difference between the Muslim and the Christian world. Since Muslim propagandists in this country persistently deny that women are inferior to men in Islam it is worth while to set out the facts. Sūra 4:31 says: 'Men have authority over women because God has made the one superior to the other and because they spend their wealth [to maintain them]. So good women are obedient, guarding the unseen [parts] because God has guarded [them]. As for those from whom you fear disobedience admonish [them] and banish them to beds apart and beat them; then if they obey you seek not occasion against them.' To a Muslim who takes his stand on the law of Islam the gulf is unbridgeable, but in actual practice in the civilized communities of the Muslim world a more liberal view of women's place in human society is gradually coming to the fore. But more on this later.

From time to time newspapers have much to say about the *jihād* or 'holy war'. Twice in the writer's lifetime efforts have been made without success to invoke it against this country and at the present time it is a dead letter, though that may not always be so. However, the texts which urge the Muslims to fight in the way of God quite obviously refer to the soil of Arabia, and though Jews and Christians are mentioned it is not at all clear whether all are included. Whether that be so or not, they are simply to be fought until they pay tribute. A moment's reflexion is sufficient to show that a *jihād* against a Western power – as opposed to local armed resistance – is impossible; a *jihād* in alliance with a non-Muslim power or powers is not a *jihād* at all, and Muslims are well aware that it is not.

Yet this question raises a most important matter which the Muslim community will have to deal with sooner or later, namely, how much of the Qurān is binding on Muslims for all time and how much was intended to apply to the prophet's age and the circumstances in which he lived. Every Muslim who has read the prophet's biography knows that much of the Qurān came into being to meet a definite crisis or occasion in Muhammad's career; but who knows whether the statutes, recommendations, prohibitions, and admonitions were intended to govern the lives of millions destined to live in conditions undreamed of in the seventh century A.D.? To take but one example: how could a Muslim keep the fast of Ramadān from sunrise to sunset in the Arctic Circle where in the summer the sun never sets? The question is further complicated by the doctrine of abrogation within the Qurān itself, and more especially in the writings of Muslim theologians and legists. For instance, sūra 5:85 says: 'You will surely find that the nearest in affection to believers are those who say, We are Christians' (quite obviously this applied – and still applies – to some only); and 2:59 says, 'Believers, Jews, Christians, and Sābians – whosoever believes in God and the Last Day and does what is right – they shall have their reward with their Lord, they have nothing to be afraid of and shall not be grieved.' But tradition, while leaving the first text unimpaired, asserts that the second is cancelled by 3:79, which runs: 'He who chooses a religion other than Islam, it will not be accepted from him, and in the next world he will be one of the lost.' But here it is only fair to say that the commentators rather than the Qurān are at fault, because, as we have shown above, in Muhammad's view uncorrupted Judaism and Christianity were early manifestations of Islam; and this is yet another example of Muhammad's tolerance exceeding that of many of his followers.

The Qurān is one of the world's classics which cannot be translated without grave loss. It has a rhythm of peculiar beauty and a cadence that charms the ear. Many Christian Arabs speak of its style with warm admiration, and most Arabists acknowledge its excellence. When it is read aloud or recited it has an almost hypnotic effect that makes the listener indifferent to its sometimes strange syntax and its sometimes, to us, repellent content. It is this quality it possesses of silencing criticism by the sweet music of its language that has given birth to the dogma of its inimitability; indeed it may be affirmed that within the literature of the Arabs, wide and fecund as it is both in poetry and in elevated prose, there is nothing to compare with it.

For the pious Muslim it is the holy of holies. It must never rest beneath other books, but always on the top of them; one must never drink or smoke when it is being read aloud, and it must be listened to in silence. It is a talisman against disease and disaster. In many places children under ten years of age are required to learn by heart its 6200 odd verses. They accomplish this prodigious feat at the expense of their reasoning faculty, for often their minds are so stretched by the effort of memory that they are little good for serious thought. Where there are schools of a modern type it is common to require a selection of passages rather than the whole book to be committed to memory.

There is something impressive and touching in the sight of simple people murmuring the sacred text as they travel by tram or train. In sickness the Qurān is the Muslim's standby. Friends and relatives will enter the sick-chamber and recite the Fātiha and the Throne verse. Some people never leave their homes without having a small copy of the Qurān on their person. The bereaved find their great consolation in reading it. No event of consequence in family or public life passes without the reading of an appropriate passage.

Nowadays in Cairo there is a regular item on the radio which consists of two half-hour recitations of the Qurān which can be heard in the street, the café, the home, and the hospital, calling men to think of the next world. These are followed by the faithful sometimes in rapt silence, sometimes with loud pious ejaculations.

Muslims are prone to quote verses from the Qurān in all the manifold circumstances of life. A brief anthology of these will serve both to give some idea of the content of the book and also to illustrate the deep religious feeling of the pious Muslim to whom Allāh is a living reality to an extent that the conventional European Christian will never understand. The words 'In the name of Allāh, the Compassionate, the Merciful', with which every sūra but one in the Qurān begins, are frequently used at the beginning of an undertaking, not only when a person is about to perform a religious duty, but before eating, entering a vehicle or a house, or to avert misfortune. Another verse which is very frequently recited at the end of ritual prayer, and inscribed on tombstones and religious buildings is: 'Allāh: there is no God but He, the living, the ever-existent One. Neither slumber nor sleep taketh Him. His is what the heaven and earth contain. Who can intercede with Him save by His permission? He knows what is before and behind men. They can grasp only that part of His knowledge which He wills. His throne is as wide as heaven and earth and the preservation of them wearies Him not, and He is the Exalted, the Immense.' In moments of danger people exclaim: 'God is the best protector and He is the most merciful of the merciful.' In moments of anxiety and doubt the faithful exclaim: 'Do not hearts become tranquil in remembering God?' An expression of adoration which is sometimes put to another use by those who are passing a church or hear the sound of bells, or are present at some Christian function is: 'Say: Praise belongs to God who has not taken a son, and has no associate in His kingdom, and [needs] no patron to defend Him from humiliation. Proclaim His greatness!' In imploring divine guidance at the beginning of an undertaking men say, 'And remember thy Lord when thou forgettest, and say: It may be that my Lord will guide me to a nearer way of truth than this.' Verses signifying faith and hope which the Muslim brotherhood have incorporated in their ritual are: 'O God, Sovereign of the Kingdom, Thou givest the kingdom to whom Thou wilt and takest the kingdom from whom Thou wilt. Thou exaltest and abasest whom Thou wilt. In Thy hand is good. Thou art able to do all things. Thou causest the night to pass into the day and the day to pass into the night. Thou bringest forth the living from the dead and the dead from the living. And Thou givest sustenance to whom Thou wilt without reckoning.'

A great many verses almost of a proverbial nature are frequently cited, such as 'God does not charge a soul with more than it can bear'; 'No soul will bear the burden of another'; 'Keep to forgiveness and enjoin kindness and turn away from the ignorant, and if an evil suggestion from Satan trouble thee seek refuge in God. He is the Hearing, the Knowing.' A phrase common when a Muslim fears that he may transgress one of the food taboos is: 'But whosoever is constrained [to eat it] without [intending to be] a rebel or transgressor incurs no guilt.' Pathetic words spoken in the Qurān by Jacob to his unsympathetic sons, 'I complain unto God of my sorrow and sadness', are often used by the faithful in sorrows of life, and a formula of resignation in death or before a dreaded disaster is: 'We belong to God and to Him we return.'

Some texts enjoin faith in God's purpose in the world in spite of its evils, and encourage men to hope for better things, such as; 'Do not think that God is unmindful of those who act unjustly'; 'Do not despair of God's spirit. Only unbelieving men despair of God's spirit.' 'Do not think that God will break His promise to His apostles. God is Powerful and vengeance is His.' This is a favourite text with the Muslim brotherhood. 'Covet not the advantage which God has given to some over others' is an injunction which needs no comment. Beggars, who often quote phrases from the Qurān, are particularly fond of the text 'Good deeds put to flight evil ways.' Not so edifying is the quotation from Potiphar's words: 'Your guile is great indeed!' which is often addressed to women. A verse which makes a great appeal to courteous and liberal-minded Muslims will make a fitting end to this anthology: 'Call men to the way of thy Lord with wisdom and goodly exhortation. Dispute with them in the most excellent way.'

CHAPTER FOUR

THE ISLAMIC EMPIRE

THE purpose of this chapter is to give the reader a brief outline of the history of the Islamic Empire, so that he may have
some idea of the shape of the events which gave the Islamic
countries the form they have today. As we have seen, Islam
was born when the two great empires of the Near and Middle
East had exhausted one another in a long series of wars. The
Byzantines were hated by their Semitic and Coptic subjects
because of their oppressive taxation and their persecution of
the 'heretic' churches. They were, after all, interlopers in the
Semitic world, heirs of a different culture and language. The
situation in the Persian empire was somewhat similar. Many
rivals to the Zoroastrianism of the state raised their heads and
were kept down only by an army of mercenaries whose
loyalty was seldom above suspicion. Thus neither of the
great powers of the time was in a position to offer an effective
resistance to the new enemy. Their border-lands were inhabited by people sympathetic to the Arabs, people who had
groaned for years under their tyranny and desired only to be
rid of it. The Christianity common to the Orthodox and the
Monophysites in the Byzantine sphere was no longer a binding force, and in the Persian sphere the Christian population
had little or nothing to lose by a change of masters. As soon
as the money which had commanded the services of the
Arab frontier guards was withdrawn this powerful striking
force threw in its lot with the newcomers.

We will now look briefly at the infant Muslim community to see how it behaved when it was deprived by death of its

revered head. By a *coup d'état* Abū Bakr, the faithful friend of Muhammad, was elected Caliph – the word *khalīfa* means 'deputy' or 'representative' – to the chagrin of the Medinan and Meccan parties. The new régime was extraordinarily successful; indeed its success for a time concealed the underlying disunion which gave birth to schisms in the body politic which have never been healed. Abū Bakr had to take action against a widespread rebellion among the Arab tribesmen, who, thinking that their link with Islam was broken by the death of the man to whom they had given their allegiance, refused to pay the alms tax or to give any heed to the treaties to which they were parties. The Caliph immediately attacked them, and from the campaigns thus begun there developed almost by accident the attack on the settled lands to the east, north, and west.

The dominant figure in these conquests was Khālid ibn al-Walīd, whose descendants lived in Jerusalem until the last few years. This man is famous for his march from Iraq across the Syrian desert to Damascus, which he sacked in A.D. 634. A Byzantine army forced the Arabs to withdraw from the town, but two years later the Arabs inflicted such a disastrous defeat on the Byzantines that all Syria and Palestine lay open to them with the exception of Jerusalem and Caesarea. Three years earlier Khālid had raided Hīra, the Persian outpost, and discovered the unpreparedness of the land. After a serious setback the Arabs defeated the Persians at Qādisīya, captured the ancient capital of Ctesiphon, and gained possession of the whole of Iraq. None of these victories would have been possible had the population been hostile to the invaders.

Egypt offered an even easier field of conquest. There the Byzantines were hated as nowhere else, and a small force of less than 10,000 men captured in 640 the whole of Lower

Egypt with the exceptions of the fortified town of Babylon near Cairo, and of Alexandria, which fell a year or two later.

The pattern of the Arab occupation took shape somewhat on these lines. Garrison towns generally on the edge of the desert were occupied or formed when there was no existing town there, and these became the centres of Arab government. To them the inhabitants of the country came to market their produce and wares, and through them the knowledge of Arabic gradually permeated the country. All non-Muslims had to pay a tax, and this disability not unnaturally led to a vast access of converts to Islam. Such converts theoretically became Arabs by attaching themselves as clients (*mawālī*) to some Arab tribe. These towns housed a large number of civilian employees from the occupied country, and they performed such services as a military community requires of its civilian dependants. The policy of the ruling class was to allow the natives to administer the country very much as they had always done. However there was a warning of things to come when 'Umar, the second Caliph, declared that the whole of the new empire was the property of the Muslim community. Certain lands were declared to be State property, and existing landowners were allowed to hold the land on payment of a tax. Thus from the beginning there was a marked difference between the Arabs and the indigenous populations of the conquered countries: the latter, if they were Jews or Christians, were taken under the protection of the Muslims because they were members of tolerated religions. Jewish and Christian writers of this time express their satisfaction at the milder rule of the Arabs and thank God for their deliverance from the tyranny of Byzantium.

When 'Umar was murdered a council elected 'Uthmān as

his successor. This man, who had a reputation for running away from battle, was a member of one of the ruling families of Mecca, and his appointment spelt the ruin of the hopes of the Medinans, who had contributed everything to the success of the prophet. With his appointment the old Meccan aristocracy saw their opportunity, and they got him to appoint members of their families to the highest posts in the empire to such an extent that armed rebellion broke out, and 'Uthmān was murdered at Medina. 'Alī, the fourth and last of the so-called Rightly Guided Caliphs, was elected to succeed him. From that moment a schism which has never been healed occurred in the Arab world, and indeed in Islam itself. 'Alī was opposed by 'Ā'isha, the prophet's widow, and by two Meccans called Talha and Zubayr. He defeated them in an engagement which is known as the 'battle of the Camel' and the two leaders were killed. But this was but the beginning of his troubles. Mu'āwiya, whom 'Uthmān had appointed governor of Syria, was the nephew of the murdered Caliph, and he demanded vengeance for his blood in such a way as to imply, though not roundly to assert, that he held him responsible for his death, or at any rate for the immunity of his murderers. How far 'Alī was in fact responsible it is difficult to determine. He was not energetic in defending him. 'Alī deposed Mu'āwiya, but the latter ignored his orders, and 'Alī was compelled to take the field against him. The battle that followed at Siffīn on the Euphrates was indecisive. The Syrians got the worst of the fighting, but by a trick they brought hostilities to an end: they fixed copies or leaves of the Qurān on the point of their lances, shouting, 'Let Allah decide!' Much against his will 'Alī was forced by the devout Muslims in his army to adopt arbitration. This so angered a fanatical party who asserted that one who held the position of Caliph could not submit his claims to arbitration that they left him. They were known as the Seceders (*Khā-rijites*, see Ch. 6). 'Alī had to exert great efforts in suppressing them. Meanwhile the arbitration went against him, but he refused to abide by it. His power was curtailed when Mu'āwiya snatched Egypt from his grasp, and when he was murdered by a Khārijite in 661 his son resigned any rights he may have had to Mu'āwiya, who became the first Caliph of the Umayyad dynasty.

Almost all the works of Arab historians which have come down to us were written when the 'Abbāsids, the dynasty which succeeded the Umayyads, were in power, and so their enormous service to the Islamic community in carrying it from the Atlantic to India and carving out a kingdom in Europe itself was ignored, and they were branded as impious usurpers and enemies of the true religion of the prophet. Only in recent years under the influence of the researches of Arabists has there been any recognition among Muslims of the debt which everywhere they owe to the Umayyads. They were Arabs first and last. The dynasty that followed them was Arab in name, but it relied on the *mawālī* or client peoples for its support. As soon as the great wave of Arab expansion had spent itself, dissension and civil war broke out among the Arabs, and before the end of the seventh century it was clear that the dynasty could not endure. A small number of Arabs were battening on the millions of the conquered peoples. Most of these were soldiers or officials. An Egyptian source gives the number of Arab peasants in Egypt towards the end of the Umayyad period as 3000.

Among the many causes which led to the downfall of the Arab kingdom the greatest was the resentment of the *mawālī* at their social and economic inferiority. They paid more taxes than the Muslims, their theoretical brethren. However blue the blood that ran in their veins they were subject to a sort of colour bar. They were not permitted to marry Arab women, and if some did, their union was regarded much as mixed marriages are today. Even when they fought in the Arab armies, as thousands of them did, they were paid less than their Arab comrades and had a smaller share in the booty. Before very long they outnumbered the true-born Arab in the towns and settlements and formed a dangerous element in the State. Their social grievance was patent. They were heirs of a higher culture. It was their knowledge of the arts of civilization which had given the Arabs a higher standard of life while their economic disabilities became more and more irksome. These people formed the backbone of the Shī'a opposition, in origin an Arab party, which centred in Iraq.

A coalition was formed when Abū Hāshim, a descendant of 'Alī but not through Fātima the prophet's daughter, resigned his claim to the caliphate in favour of a descendant of 'Abbās, one of the prophet's uncles. The base of the new movement was in Khurāsān. This man's son Ibrāhīm gathered an army which was largely recruited in Persia, and sweeping all before it defeated and destroyed the Umayyads on the banks of the Zāb and Abū'l-'Abbās became Caliph in 750.

The results of this change were enormous. Iraq, not Syria, was now the centre of the empire, and a strong middle class came into being, while lawyers and theologians acquired an importance they had never enjoyed under the old régime. The taunt that theirs was a kingdom rather than a caliphate would be better levelled at the 'Abbāsids, for in the days of their power they were not men who could be approached in the familiar Arab way like the Umayyads, but monarchs surrounded by a host of officials and underlings whom those seeking audience must bribe to gain admittance to the Caliph's presence. Society was not altogether unlike that familiar to the English reader in *The Arabian Nights*, though he must remember that in that book of popular stories he is reading a caricature of the past. Some of the world's most impious and tyrannical rulers were numbered among these 'Abbāsids, who with one or two exceptions paid lip-service to Islam and gave their official support to the innovations which came in under the guise of a return to apostolic custom and practice. At the height of 'Abbāsid power their subjects enjoyed a period of unexampled economic prosperity. Trade by land and sea was developed to an amazing degree; agriculture and irrigation were developed, and the arts and sciences were cultivated as never before. Arab supremacy survived in the Arabic language, but it would hardly be an exaggeration to call this the period of Persian dominance. But in less than a century the unity of this imposing empire began to dissolve: Persia, Spain, Morocco, Tunisia, and Egypt broke away under independent rulers, and in the middle of the tenth century the Buwayhids, a Persian dynasty, invaded Baghdād and reduced the Caliphs to mere puppets, nominally heads of Church and State but possessing no power whatever.

Among the many powers that rose on the ruins of the 'Abbāsid empire one of the most important was the Fātimid dynasty in Egypt. The tenets of the Ismā'īlīs are described in Ch. 6. The Fātimids came to power as the result of the success of Ismā'īlī propaganda in Tunisia. There is more than a trace of communism in their original teaching and practice, but when they gained political supremacy they were not very different from their predecessors. The Fātimids built Cairo, and the world-famous mosque of al-Azhar was their religious centre. It did not become the great centre of orthodox Islamic teaching until later. At the height of their power these Caliphs governed the whole of North Africa, Sicily, Egypt, Syria, and Western Arabia. They went the way of their rivals in Baghdad, and were suppressed by Saladin, who brought Egypt under the sway of orthodox Islam once more.

The Muslim entry into Europe began with sporadic raids on outlying islands such as Cyprus and Rhodes. These became more and more serious until in the ninth century the Arabs gained possession of Sicily. From these outposts they raided the mainland and threatened Rome itself. The history of Sicily under the Normans, who held the island from the end of the eleventh to the end of the twelfth century, shows an extraordinary intermingling of Muslim and Christian culture. Spain was conquered, save for the extreme north, and held by the Muslims from the eighth to the fifteenth century, by which time their territory had been reduced to a mere fragment of the country. They have left an indelible mark on the language and literature of the Peninsula. Here as in the old Byzantine empire the Arabs were at first welcomed as deliverers from the intolerable yoke of Church and State, and thousands of the inhabitants accepted Islam. Such a hold had Arab civilization gained that it was found necessary to translate the Bible and Liturgy into Arabic for the use of the Christian community. Scholars from the West visited Spain to learn philosophy, mathematics, astronomy, and medicine. The oldest European universities owe an enormous debt to those scholars who returned from Spain bringing with them the knowledge they had gained at the Arab universities of that country.

While William the Conqueror was establishing his authority in England the empire of the Arabs was breaking up. The Turks in the East, the Christians in the West, and the Berbers in Africa were paving the way for its dissolution and decay. Thanks to these causes the Crusaders were able to establish their transient and ill-fated rule in the Holy Land. The less said about the land-grabbing venture of the Crusades the better. In itself it was but a passing incident, with little or no permanent effect. Its one lasting result was to embitter for ever, it would seem, the relations between Christians and Muslims, and to bring misery on successive generations of Eastern Christians who were left to bear the brunt of Muslim resentment. One contemporary Arab writer looked upon the Franks as little better than ignorant beasts, and gives some blood-curdling examples of their surgery and superstitious practices in medicine, and their trials by ordeal; he notes the civilizing influence which residence in the East has on them. On the other hand, he admits that some of them were loyal and kindly friends. Another Arab writer laments the injustice and rapacity of Muslim rulers and landlords, and speaks of the mildness of Frankish rule and their justice 'on which one can always depend'.

In the thirteenth century Arab civilization suffered a blow from which it has never entirely recovered. Jenghīz Khān led his Mongols across the Oxus, and when he died left his grandson Hūlāgu to carry on his work. He shattered the Persians, captured Baghdād, and put the petty Caliph to death in 1258. The Turk Baybars defeated the Mongols and established a line of 'Abbāsid caliphs in Cairo with the title only; they possessed no real power. This Mamlūk sultanate founded by Baybars lasted until 1517, when the Ottoman Turks overthrew them and remained masters of Syria, Egypt, and most of Arabia until our own day. The Ottoman Sultan Selim carried off Mutawakkil, the last of the Caliphs, to Constantinople, and himself assumed the title of Caliph.

By this time the Turks had carved out an empire in eastern Europe. The fifth centenary of their capture of Constantinople was celebrated in 1953; their westward march was not checked until they reached the walls of Vienna. For nearly five hundred years the Arab world stagnated. No creative writer or thinker appeared among the Arabs, and they were not awakened from their slumber until the Western nations appeared in the East. But now we have reached the modern era.

CHAPTER FIVE

APOSTOLIC TRADITION

WITH the death of the prophet authoritative direction as from on high came to an abrupt end. If the community was to hold together, guidance in all the changing conditions of life had to be provided. The Qurān, of course, where it could be invoked, was the final authority; but even that demanded authoritative explanation. In all religious communities professional theologians are to be found. Such men are compelled by force of circumstances, or take it on themselves, to define what a man must believe and do in order to live as a faithful member of his church. In Islam these duties are defined perhaps even more meticulously than in the Jewish Talmud and to a far greater extent than any ordinary European would suppose possible. Thus, for example, precise details governing the washing of the hands, head, and beard, rinsing of the mouth, nostrils, and ears, and the use of dust or sand when water is not procurable are prescribed and obligatory; the kind of clothes and personal ornaments persons may or may not wear; the way they should salute each other, and so on, are all subject to religious law and not matters of personal preference, though, of course, great latitude in some of these matters is common in many Muslim countries today.

Readers of the Qurān will perceive that the laws which govern Muslim custom (*sunna*) in these everyday affairs are adumbrated there, but they will look in vain for the details which make these customs into formal rites and rules of behaviour. To find the underlying authority for these rules we must go to the books of tradition (*hadīth*). In theory the life of the individual Muslim is governed by what the prophet said and did; in fact by what he is reported to have said and done; and the two are not always the same. Exactly when records of the deeds and words of the prophet were first written down we do not know; indeed early tradition is at variance with itself on this very point. Some say that the prophet authorized the writing of his sayings; others assert that he forbade it. At any rate it is certain that several small collections of traditions were assembled in Umayyad times.

So strong was the force of Muslim feeling that in the third century A.H. it was deemed necessary to establish the principle that law, custom, and belief should rest upon the practice of the prophet and his Companions and Followers. People who were vitally concerned were, of course, lawyers, and so many of the early books on tradition were collections of sayings which could be used by judges and others as a guide in framing laws and regulating society. Other principles which will be discussed later influenced the lawyers, but the earliest law book to survive, the *Muwatta* of Mālik ibn Anas (d. A.H. 179), though it contains many traditions, does not show that indisputable mark of the later *hadīth* literature—the chain of authorities which carry back the tradition to the prophet himself and guarantee its authenticity. This is always in the form 'A told me that B said that C had informed him that D related that he heard E say I heard F ask the apostle of God about . . . (or say that the apostle said . . .)'

It will be obvious that if an individual or a group or a sect wanted to establish its right to its beliefs or practices, it had to furnish proof that the prophet had authorized its course of action or its attitude. In consequence, an enormous number of *hadīth* soon found their way into circulation, and it soon became apparent that forgery on a large scale was at work everywhere. There were traditions in favour of the ruling house, of the rival claims to the caliphate; there were commendations of quietists and condemnation of the sit-at-homes; there were contradictory traditions on a host of subjects. If this state of affairs were to continue the Muslim state would be in danger of social anarchy.

So great was the veneration for Muhammad that once his name was invoked with a chain of authorities going back through his 'companions' and 'helpers' to the prophet himself, the ordinary Muslim was reluctant to reject the tradition lest he should be thought guilty of disrespect to his great leader. Nevertheless, by the third century, action had become imperative, and a critical school had come into being with certain clearly marked principles of criticism. Unfortunately they directed their attention not so much towards the intrinsic probability of the tradition, or to current practice based on precedent demonstrably early, as to the character of the reporters and the circumstances of their lives. Biographies which set forth the number of facts in the career of early Muslims, the dates and times at which they lived, the places they visited, and so on, provided some sort of check on the statement that A told B. Obviously if it came to be shown that A died when B was a baby, the tradition was a forgery. If A lived at one end of the Islamic empire and D at the other, it would have to be proved that they had ever met. Occasionally it is said roundly that a transmitter was a liar or an untrustworthy person, but seldom does this charge rest on the nature of his report – as, for instance, that he saw the moon split – unless the report is disliked because it cuts across a common and agreed practice of the community or is repugnant to the dominant school of thought. As a result of these labours, traditions came to be divided into three categories, 'genuine', 'good', and 'weak', but as the science of tradition developed, at least fifty more terms were employed to mark different classes of tradition.

The first collection to gain, and ever after hold, canonical authority was the *Saḥīḥ* (the genuine) of al-Bukhārī (A.H. 194–256), to all intents and purposes really a collection of proof tests for lawyers, though other matters are dealt with. Bukhārī's biographer says that he selected his material from no less than 600,000 *ḥadīth*. If we allow for repetitions which occur under different heads, he reduced this vast number of forgeries or dubious reports to less than 3000 *ḥadīth*. In other words, less than one in every 200 traditions which circulated in his day could pass his test.

The Muslim conception of law being so much more comprehensive than ours, it could not be argued that the later collections which embody a mass of material not to be found in the *Saḥīḥ* contain traditions with which Bukhārī was not concerned, though exception might be made perhaps in the case of traditions on some matters which are not discussed, or receive but scant notice, in his book. There will always be some difference of opinion on a matter of subjective judgement, but nevertheless (*a*) accusations of forgery are so frequent in Arabic writers, (*b*) so many traditions are demonstrably false, (*c*) so many can be proved to be of later origin, that it is hardly possible to be too critical of what is left; moreover, many are obviously of foreign origin, particularly Jewish, and in a lesser degree Christian. Some even ultimately owe their origin to the philosophers of Greece. However, it is interesting to note that the principal early grammarians, though they dare not say that the *ḥadīth* were not authentic, asserted that the Arabic in which they were written was so bad that they could not be held to transmit the actual words of the prophet, though doubtless they conveyed his meaning. Their argument was that it is impossible that the prophet, the exponent of perfect Arabic, could have violated the rules of grammar. However, it is doubtful if this somewhat sweeping statement could be applied to all the *hadīth*, and there are grounds for believing that the style of some of them is true to early Arab usage.

But it must not be supposed that the early Arab empire had no law until the first collections of apostolic tradition were compiled. Law follows custom either by canonizing it or by correcting and regulating it. Consequently we must look for its genesis and evolution in the principal cities and centres of administration. The first four caliphs carried on and adapted the practice of their master, but already social and administrative problems for which there was no precedent confronted them, and they had to issue directives. To some extent they were guided by the *sunna*, the old way of life which they had inherited from their forefathers, and subsequently their decisions became a part of the *sunna* of their successors; and, later still, the practice of the Umayyad government was also regarded as the *sunna*. Last of all, as we shall see later, traditions were invented to show that everything that a Muslim was required to believe and do was founded on traditions purporting to prove that Muhammad, by example or precept, had so ruled. Thus *sunna* was first ancient custom, then contemporary, immediate past practice, and finally the ideal behaviour of the prophet as enshrined in tradition.

Muhammadan jurisprudence may be said to have started with the second century A.H. At this time provincial governors were the administrators of justice, local judges acting as their appointed agents. It is clear, for example, from the statement of St John of Damascus that flogging was the punishment for theft that the commandment in the Qurān which ordered that the hand of the thief should be cut off was set aside. Penal and military laws were less strict under the Umayyads than under their successors. Vast territories were being conquered, and amid the pressing problems created by incessant wars, the financing of the empire, the different languages spoken in the conquered countries, and the settling of the hordes of land-hungry Arabs it would be folly to expect that a code of law could be drawn up, or, if it were drawn up, administered systematically in the circumstances that prevailed. 'The system that had sufficed to guard the right to a few sheep or camels had to be transformed before it would suffice to adjust the rights and claims of a tribe of millionaires.' One cannot but admire the achievements of the Umayyads, who not only founded the Islamic empire, but established in broad outline the shape it has assumed ever since.

Their successors, the 'Abbāsids, who practically exterminated the ruling family, encouraged the legend of their godlessness and indifference to the laws of Islam and found no difficulty in pointing out their shortcomings. Though there was substance in their charges, they and the host of poets, lawyers, theologians, and courtiers entirely ignored the difficult conditions of the Umayyad age. The new Caliphs were careful to keep away from Syria and to make their new capital in Iraq, where they lived luxuriously on the proceeds of the conquests of their predecessors.

Unfortunately the earliest law books or collections of traditions of the prophet's behaviour, such as that of Ibn Ishāq, the prophet's biographer (died A.H. 150), have perished. All we know of the book is that it differed materially from those of his younger contemporaries. Indeed, incidents in the life of the prophet, which he records apparently without any *arrière pensée*, are rejected by later lawyers actually because they would form a precedent contrary to current practice or to the opinion of those lawyers as to what the law ought to be. Short of branding a man a liar – and some did not boggle at that – the only way to discredit a tradition was to say that it emanated from an unreliable source – or, as some jurisprudents required, lacked the authority of the prophet himself and was but the statement of one of his Companions.

It is much to be regretted that the first Islamic law books have long since perished. We have little at first hand from the earliest authorities in the Hijaz, Syria, or Iraq, so that there is some dispute as to the area in which Islamic jurisprudence originated. On the one hand we have the unequivocal statement of the prophet's biographer Ibn Ishāq that Medina is 'the home of the *sunna*'; a fact of considerable importance, because when he dictated his book or gave his lectures he was a subject of the 'Abbāsid Caliph living in Iraq. From the context it would seem to follow that in his opinion it was Medina and Medina alone where primitive practice was known and followed. On the other hand it is obvious that the Arab empire could not wait for the opinion of the jurists of Medina, even if they attached paramount importance to it, and there is no evidence that they did; and so we find systems of law springing up in all the principal centres of Islamic rule under the guidance of individual jurisprudents.

The essential feature common to all ancient schools of law was the living tradition in current Umayyad practice. Within this essential unity there was wide diversity – not so much geographical, as one would expect, as personal, expressed in adherence to the opinions of an outstanding exponent of the law. At the present day these differences have been enormously reduced in the great legal schools, to one of which lawyers must belong, though they are still numerous and occasionally seriously affect a man's social life. A study of the earliest law books reveals facts of paramount practical importance: the earliest writers such as Mālik in Medina regarded decisions, or acts, or words, of the prophet's Companions, or the next generation called the Followers, as binding only when they were in accord with the practice of the community; the great systematizer and reformer al-Shāfiʿī refused to accept any traditions as legally valid but those which purported to hold the prophet's authority. The number of this category of traditions enormously increased between al-Shāfiʿī (d. A.H. 204) and Ibn Māja (d. A.H. 273).

But first let us look at the early lawyer at work. He was well acquainted with local tradition and practice; he knew the Qurān by heart, and some of the traditions which ran with, or sometimes apart from, the *sunna*. A case came up for decision which no precedent and no text had dealt with. If he gave judgement with nothing to guide him but his own sense of justice, it was called 'opinion'; if he was able to argue from a general premise derived from some other case with a real or imaginary common factor, the decision was said to be based on 'analogy'. Other sub-categories were 'personal preference' and 'public weal'. Later developments severely restricted the operation of these subjective factors by the multiplication of traditions which either gave them the authority of apostolic tradition or contradicted them by the same means.

The ordinary reader would find it tedious to trace the

intricate and involved history of the course of law during the Umayyad period, and so we will pass direct to the founder of the classical theory of Muslim law, al-Shāfi'ī (A.H. 150–204). According to his theory law is based on four principles: the Qurān; the words and deeds of the prophet (*sunna*); the catholic consent of the community (*ijmā'*); and analogy (*qiyās*). Up to his day the living tradition in the principal towns was largely dependent on the opinion of the most prominent lawyer they had produced, though it was often subject to rival interpretations. Though there was of course a firm stratum of tradition common everywhere, there was no logical and consistent system into which divergent practices could be fitted and no satisfactory basis for them. Shāfi'ī's fundamental principle was that nothing could supersede or set aside a tradition, properly authenticated, which could be traced back to the prophet himself. Such a tradition invalidated anything to the contrary which had been said or done by any Companion, even one of the rightly guided Caliphs. Shāfi'ī was not the first to put forward this idea of seeking the prophet's authority for a desired enactment. Long before he was born, according to the author of the prophet's biography, it was claimed that the prophet on his death-bed had said that two religions should not coexist in Arabia. Abū Bakr, who of all men would have been sure to know the truth, did nothing to carry out the alleged dying command of Muhammad, and 'Umar said that he had never heard a word of it; but when he was assured that Muhammad had indeed uttered these words he proceeded to expel Jews and Christians from the Hijāz. We can see quite plainly how this new insistence on a definite tradition going back to the prophet influenced both the fabrication of *isnād*, the chain of transmitters, and *matn*, the subject-matter of the tradition.

Shāfiʿī in his youth was familiar with a certain tradition, but it stopped short at ʿUmar. Later he heard it on Muhammad's authority by another *isnād*. From what he says it can be seen what an untrustworthy guide to ancient practice tradition (*hadīth*) had become in Shāfiʿī's day, half a century before the first, and in many ways most important, collector of apostolic tradition died. Where there were two properly authenticated traditions from the prophet which could not be reconciled, what was to be done? If one was known to repeal the other, all was well: it was on a par with those verses of the Qurān which have an abrogating authority. If one was more trustworthy it was to be followed; if they were equally trustworthy the one closer to the Qurān and the *sunna* of the prophet was to be followed. Tradition from other persons could neither establish nor contradict an apostolic tradition. Shāfiʿī's attitude of mind is characteristically Arabian. In some cases ingenuity could produce harmony, but sometimes even he had to say that a tradition which he could not or would not accept was unreliable.

This fundamental thesis of Shāfiʿī gave a violent twist to the development of the *shariʿa*, the sacred law, by cutting it off from its historic past. There was no recognition of the likelihood that the law as it was when he took it in hand was the practice of the primitive community sanctioned by the prophet's silence on matters which that wise statesman left to his countrymen to settle by pursuing the customs of their forefathers and leaving their posterity to formulate laws to deal with problems as they arose. By his elaboration of the supreme authority of *hadīth*, Shāfiʿī placed it on a par with the Qurān itself, and when he made it the authoritative interpretation of the heavenly book, in effect he gave it a higher authority. God had made obedience to the prophet incumbent on all believers, and therefore what he said came from God as the Qurān did. Thus divine authority invests a canonical tradition.

This doctrine put Islam into a strait jacket which, if it were accepted with all its implications – and it never was – would make all development in Muslim society impossible. It also corrupted it from within, for once Shāfiʿī's principle was accepted the only way to enforce a new law or validate existing practice was to invent a tradition with an *isnād* which conformed to the accepted pattern. Shāfiʿī was a man of the highest integrity, but, as we have seen, he was fully aware of the existence of spurious traditions, though he would admit their existence only when every effort to harmonize them with others that were judged trustworthy, or to explain them away, had been exhausted. But he placed a dangerous weapon in the hands of his successors. The process of stiffening and hardening the legal system of Islam was carried through. The old and comparatively elastic régime of the Umayyads, which, apart from certain obvious but unimportant departures from qurānic legislation, faithfully represented the mild reasonableness of Muhammad's rule, was replaced by a rigid unbending code of law which in spirit was opposed to the whole tenor of his life and thought, and yet claimed, by the theft of his name, the authority of God himself.

It may well be thought that this is a serious allegation, and therefore something must be said to substantiate it. In the first place, it cannot be denied that the oldest authorities on apostolic tradition paid little attention to the *isnād*. Indeed there was no reason why they should. When they wrote or lectured on the life of the prophet either for edification or for instructing their hearers, there was often someone present who knew as much as they did on a particular incident or saying. What they said was common knowledge among those who had lived with the men whom they claimed as their informants. Neither Ibn Ishāq nor Wāqidī nor Mālik nor Auzā'ī (d. A.H. 157) cared much about a chain of authorities. Sometimes they cited them in full; sometimes they stopped short at a Companion; sometimes they quoted a Successor, i.e. an authority of the second generation; sometimes they think it sufficient to say that one of the traditionists told them something and do not think it necessary to state his name. Historically, therefore, a theoretically faulty *isnād* is the mark of an ancient tradition; and conversely, an unexceptionable *isnād* is suspect as the invention of a later generation.

Secondly, it is clear from Mālik's attitude to *hadīth* that in his opinion and in the opinion of his contemporaries it had no overriding authority. When it suited them they followed it and quoted it; when it did not they disregarded it, whether it went back to the prophet or to a Companion. On the whole they seem to have preferred traditions from Companions to traditions from the prophet. There they must surely have been working on the right lines. The Companions would have cited the prophet's example. The historic Muhammad took his own decisions as occasion arose. He did not concern himself with the minutiae of business transactions and what not. He was far too occupied with the serious task of consolidating his authority in Arabia and attracting its inhabitants to Islam. The early authorities in the Hijāz, Iraq, and Syria are at one in holding that the Companions are the most trustworthy authorities on apostolic practice.

Thirdly, we may cite the opposition of Shāfi'ī's contemporaries who were alarmed at the growth of traditions claiming the prophet's authority. They pointed to the existence of contradictory traditions and argued that apart from the consensus of opinion of the learned and the current practice there was no ground for accepting either tradition as authentic. They could quote a tradition which said: 'If what I am reported to have said agrees with the Qurān I did say it; if it does not, I did not say it!' They maintained that Shāfiʿī's insistence and reliance on traditions from the prophet was an innovation and they opposed agreed practice to *hadīth*. When they claimed explicitly or implicitly that what had always been held and done was the *sunna* of the prophet they gave Shāfiʿī an opportunity which he seized by claiming that the *sunna* of the prophet was identical with the traditions that carried his name, and to these the community must bow.

Lastly, there is a demonstrable process of fabrication from the earliest written collections of traditions concerned with law down to the classical collections of Bukhārī, Ibn Māja (d. A.H. 273), and others. Sometimes it is merely the extension of the *isnād* of a tradition previously known and followed; at others it is something entirely new. Shāfiʿī often states explicitly that there is no tradition from the prophet on a particular point of law, which in fact is based on practice, and the required documentation duly appears in the later canonical collections.

Before the end of the second century a principle which has never been abandoned was in force, namely the doctrine of consensus or catholic consent (*ijmāʿ*). In effect it was the agreement of the *ʿulamā* or doctors in certain regions, and itself became the subject of a tradition from the prophet to the effect that his community would not agree on an error. This doctrine was and is of enormous importance. In the age when the *sharīʿa* was being fixed it marked the limit between orthodoxy and heresy and between the permitted and the forbidden. But at that time it shut the door on progress and development. When in the third century the doctors had agreed on the acceptance and interpretation of *hadīth* there was no room for criticism or amendment. The last word had been spoken. The man who exercised his own judgement (the *mujtahid*) could do so only on matters of detail which had not already been provided for, and naturally such matters grew fewer and fewer with the passage of the years. Some scholars have drawn an analogy between *ijmā'* and the oecumenical councils of the Church, and there is substance in the argument, because defiance of the consensus was branded as *bid'a*, innovation, which corresponds to heresy.

On the other hand, *ijmā'* is the one hope of the Islamic system today. Just as in the past it was able to make a dead letter of a tradition or even a qurānic text, so today it can ignore, and despite obscurantist opposition frequently has ignored, elements in the *sharī'a* which are out of line with the conditions of the modern world. See the concluding chapter.

In brief, the system which was based on the Qurān, the *sunna*, consensus, and analogy (*qiyās*, the application of a principle governing more or less parallel cases) reduced the acts of believers to five categories:

(1) Obligatory,
(2) Recommended but not obligatory,
(3) Indifferent,
(4) Disapproved but not forbidden,
(5) Prohibited.

The Muslim Sunnīs are distributed among four schools or 'ways' (*madhāhib*), the Shī'īs having their own schools. On all matters of vital importance they are in agreement, and all recognize the other systems as orthodox. Every Muslim must belong to one of these schools. The first in time, the Hanifite, is named after Abū Hanīfa (d. A.H. 150), the founder of the Iraqi school. His followers today are centred in western Asia (excluding Arabia), India, and Lower Egypt. The second is the Mālikite, named after Mālik ibn Anas (d. A.H. 179), the founder of the Madina school and the author of the first comprehensive law book to survive. His school is predominant in North and West Africa and Upper Egypt. The third is the Shāfiʿite. As we have seen, Shāfiʿī is the outstanding figure in Muslim jurisprudence, a powerful, forceful thinker with a grasp of principles and problems and a master of argument. His influence on succeeding generations was very great. His school is represented in Lower Egypt, Syria, India, and especially in Indonesia. Finally, there are the Hanbalites, followers of Ahmad b. Hanbal (d. A.H. 241). It is a strange fact, but nevertheless certain, that Ibn Hanbal did not establish a system of his own; it was left to his pupils to systematize his teaching. He was intensely conservative in the matter of *hadīth*, and in general it may be said that he was responsible for the most intolerant and fanatical view of a Muslim's duties and responsibilities. It may well be that his physical suffering at the hands of the Muʿtazila had bred a spirit of uncompromising hostility towards the use of reason in law and dogma. For centuries his school has been diminishing, but it has gained a new lease of life today in the Wahhābī kingdom.

Lastly, a word must be said about the settlement of cases not already provided for in the *sharīʿa*. The jurisconsult (*muftī*) is asked to give an opinion, and his pronouncement, called a *fatwā*, then provides the judge with material on which to base his decision, or the individual with a ruling on which to regulate his actions. Until comparatively recently the Chief Muftī of Constantinople was called the 'Shayhk of Islam', and he was the highest religious authority in the old Turkish empire. These *fatwās* are an important supplement to the text-books of the schools, since they deal with modern conditions and tell the pious Muslim how he is to shape his life in an environment which is constantly changing. Perhaps the most famous *fatwā* in Islamic history was that issued by Ibn Taymīya in the fourteenth century. He condemned the pilgrimage to tombs of saints and even to the tomb of Muhammad in Medina as a form of idolatry, and forbade the invocation of saints and prophets. More will be said about the administration of law in Muslim countries today in Chapter 9.

In theory, the Shī'ite conception of the supreme authority in law is utterly different from that of the Sunnīs, though in practice the difference does not amount to very much. They reject the four schools and the doctrine of *ijmā'* because their Hidden Imām has the sole right of determining what the believer shall do and believe. Therefore their duly accredited doctors can still exercise the power of *ijtihād* or personal opinion. This power the Sunnīs lost a thousand years ago or more. Where differences between Sunnī and Shī'ī law occur, often they are not so much specifically Shī'ī tenets as survivals of primitive Islamic custom. For example, sūra 4:28 reads: 'You are permitted in addition to seek out wives with your wealth in modest conduct but not in fornication; give them their pay for the enjoyment you have had of them as a duty.' Two of the earliest authorities on the text of the Qurān asserted that after the words 'enjoyment you have had of them' there was written 'for a specified period'. Clearly with this addition the Qurān permits what are called *mut'a* marriages, actually a form of legal prostitution. A man and woman agree to cohabit for a day or two or any short period specified and arranged between them. The man pays the woman's fee in kind or in money, and at the end of the agreed time the liaison automatically comes to an end. These significant words often appear in Shī'ī books. The Sunnīs reject both the reading and the practice it sanctions. As we should expect, the traditions are at variance. Some say that the prophet enjoyed these 'marriages': others say that he forbade them. One thing is certain, and that is that the practice was common in the second century A.H. In Shī'ī Persia today men await travellers at popular halting places to offer them 'wives' for the period of their sojourn there. However, in practice it is possible for a Sunnī to conclude such an alliance, provided that nothing is said about a time limit in the marriage contract and the divorce formula is pronounced with a time limit as soon as the contract is concluded. Such an arrangement was accepted as legal by Shāfi'ī, but he stigmatized it as *makrūh*, 'disapproved but not forbidden'.

At first sight such contracts which on the face of them legalize prostitution cannot but excite repugnance in the European reader. But, unpleasant though it is to see such an institution incorporated and recognized in a code of *religious* law, it is a frank and realistic attitude. No religion has ever succeeded in extirpating fornication. It exists everywhere, and there is no reason to suppose that in countries where it is frowned upon publicly it is less practised privately. Devout Muslims would not approve of such alliances, but realizing that fornication is an evil that cannot be suppressed, they have admitted it into their code with such safeguards as can be enforced. The man has to pay an agreed sum and the woman remains at his disposal during the term of the contract, thus making promiscuous intercourse with others impossible while the contract is in being. Moreover, and the point is most relevant, the *sharī'a* does not recognize any distinction between religious and secular law. Throughout its history and today in areas unaffected by Western institutions all a Muslim's actions are subject to the *sharī'a*, the divine and ordered highway of life, and no distinction between sacred and profane is possible.

We need not pause to look at the minor differences between Shī'ī and Sunnī law, though one matter on which they differ is of some importance to Western travellers in the east. The Shī'īs take a much stricter view of ritual purity, so that to them all Christians and Jews come into the category of the unclean. Where this principle is rigidly adhered to Christians are not allowed to enter Shī'ī mosques. I was politely warned not to try to enter the Kāzimayn mosque in Baghdad; and though it might have been possible to gain admission in the company of Shī'īs of my acquaintance I decided against making the attempt against the prevailing hostility towards Christians. I could not but contrast this prejudice unfavourably with the kindness I received from friends in Jerusalem who devoted some hours to showing me everything in their beautiful mosque, and that too on the feast of Nabī Mūsā when the mosque was reserved for the worship of believers. To the strict Shī'ī the 'people of the scriptures' are unclean, and they will not eat or drink from vessels they have used; but it is only fair to say that in most places where Europeans reside the prohibition is silently ignored. Still, under the surface the feeling that they are unclean (*najis*) persists.

Thus far we have been considering traditions which for the most part are concerned with law, but there is a vast literature of tradition which deals with events in the prophet's life, legends about biblical characters, events in the lives of the prophet's Companions, the interpretation of obscure passages in the Qurān, kindness to animals, and a host of other matters. The orthodox Muslim critics of tradition looked with a much more lenient eye on many of these traditions. If a *hadīth* was edifying and its *isnād* was suspect no serious objection was made to it. It could do good; it could not possibly do harm, and so it might as well be allowed to stand.

The most uncompromising opponents of *hadīth* were the Mu'tazilites (Ch. 7). A few extracts from a third-century writer who set himself the task of refuting their objections will serve to give some idea of the contents of the works of tradition and of the misgivings that they provoked. (The writer's attempts to resolve some of these contradictions are seldom convincing and need not be repeated here.) These it objectors said:

(*a*) You relate that the prophet said, 'One who has as much as a grain of mustard seed of pride will not enter Paradise, nor will one with a similar amount of faith go to hell.' Then you relate: 'He who says that there is no God but Allah will enter Paradise though he has committed fornication and robbery.' Fornication and robbery are of greater weight with God than a grain of pride, so here is a contradiction.

(*b*) You relate that the prophet said, 'There will be no prophet after me and no community after my community. The permitted will be what God has permitted by my mouth until the day of resurrection, and so also what he has forbidden by my mouth'; then you relate that the Messiah will descend and kill the swine, break the crosses, and add to what is permitted, and you assert that 'Ā'isha used to say, 'Say of the apostle of God "The Seal of the prophets" and do not say "There will be no prophet after me." '

(c) You say on 'Ā'isha's authority that the apostle never urinated while standing, while you relate on Hudhayfa's authority that he did.

(d) You relate that the prophet said concerning Saʻd: 'The throne [of God] quivered at his death and seventy thousand angels hastened to wash him [for burial], so that I could hardly approach his bier.' Then you relate that he said that if anyone could have escaped the punishment of the grave it would have been Saʻd, but he was so tightly compressed that his ribs broke. But how could the throne of God quiver at anyone's death? If such a thing were possible it would have been when one of the prophets died. If the throne of God were to quiver heaven and earth would quiver too. And how could such a thing happen for one who had to undergo the punishment of the grave? And how could seventy thousand angels wash him and the prophet be unable to approach his bier because of the crowd of angels?

(e) You relate a tradition from Ibn Ishāq on the ultimate authority of 'Ā'isha which is repugnant to reason and in contradiction to the Qurān, namely that she said that the verse about the stoning (of adulterers) and about ten acts of sucking by an infant (bring the child within the prohibited degrees so that his foster-mother and sister are his blood relations) was under her bed when the apostle died, and that they were so distracted by his death that a sheep entered the house and ate the page. This is in flat contradiction to the word of God: 'It is a mighty scripture: a vain thing cannot come at it from before or behind' (sūra 41:41). But how could the Qurān be mighty if a sheep ate it and made its law of none effect and destroyed the proof that it existed? And

how could God have said, 'Today I have perfected your religion for you' and then sent something to eat it? And how
could he expose revelation to the appetite of a sheep and not
command that it should be guarded and preserved? And why
did he send the commandment down when he did not want
it to be observed?

This last tradition has a special interest because there is no
trace of such a detailed ordinance in the Qurān, though the
law is laid down that foster-mothers and foster-sisters are
within the prohibited degrees (4:27). This *hadīth* which was
current in the first half of the second century shows how
traditions grew up to explain exactly what was meant by a
foster-mother. The child must be suckled at least ten times.
This was later reduced to five times. The passage belongs to
the small collection of verses which were said to have been
revealed to Muhammad but were abrogated and were not
included within the sacred pages of the Qurān. We have no
means of knowing whether the tradition is sound or not.

While it may be confidently affirmed that it is not possible
to place reliance on any *hadīth* which claims to represent the
words of the prophet, it must be understood that this holds
good of the later canonical collections. It is not true of tradition in the wider non-technical sense, that is to say reports of
what the prophet did and to a lesser degree what he said, as
they are found in the biography of the prophet written down
sometime before 150 A.H. by Muhammad ibn Isḥāq, which
have a far better claim on our confidence.

One example must suffice to show how traditions were
coined and gradually gained universal acceptance in Islam.
There is a solitary verse in the Qurān, the opening verse of
sūra 17, which reads, 'Glorious is He Who made His servant
go by night from the sacred mosque to the farther mosque

whose surroundings We have blessed that We might show him some of our signs.' Round this verse a whole literature has gathered. It has given birth to two separate legends which have been combined in an uneasy union. The first is called the night journey (*isrā'*); the second the ascension (*mi'rāj*, literally 'ladder'). For the night journey a strange winged beast, half donkey and half mule, called Burāq, on which earlier prophets used to ride, was brought to Muhammad, and it carried him to Jerusalem. There he met Abraham, Moses, and Jesus with a number of other prophets. Gabriel accompanied him. He then returned to Mecca and when he related his experiences he was greeted with derision and some of his own followers refused to credit his story. In the earliest traditions some of the reporters assert that the experience was visionary and that the prophet's body never left Mecca.

This story is followed by the account of the prophet's ascension to heaven. According to one reporter, after his arrival in Jerusalem a ladder was brought and his companion Gabriel took him up to a door in heaven which was guarded by an angel. Going on further he was shown the place of hell; its lid was removed and he saw its awful flames. The categories of sinners are often similar and sometimes in the same order as those described in the *Inferno*. In the second heaven he met Jesus and John the Baptist; in the third the patriarch Joseph; in the fourth Idrīs (Enoch); in the fifth Aaron; in the sixth Moses; in the seventh was Abraham. It was on this journey that the prophet received the command to order his followers to pray five times a day.

Thus the earliest account: but there is an enormous number of additions in the canonical collections of *hadīth*, and many of them are inconsistent with the earlier stories. For instance, it is said that Gabriel took Muhammad straight from Mecca to heaven; in other words, the night journey is separated from the ascension. Again Muhammad is said to have gone to heaven mounted on Burāq. But that must be wrong, because had he been taken by Burāq there would have been no need of a ladder. To meet the difficulty a harmonizing tradition says that Burāq was tied to the rock in Jerusalem while Muhammad mounted the ladder.

The historical genesis of this legend, as we have seen, is this solitary verse in the Qurān, and the vital point is the 'farther mosque' to which he was caused to go. For some reason or reasons which need not be gone into here it was asserted that this farther mosque was either in Jerusalem or in heaven itself. But two earlier writers who are never referred to in this connexion state that the prophet went by night from 'the farther mosque' in a place called al-Ji'rāna some fifteen kilometres from Mecca to the sacred mosque in the eighth year of the hijra. Thus there is a perfectly natural explanation of this verse in the Qurān, which expresses Muhammad's feelings of gratitude to God for having helped him to perform the pilgrimage at night at a time when the polytheists had not been excluded from its rites and when he would have compromised his position had he gone openly by day. The Muslim world keeps the feast of the Mi'rāj on the 27th of Rajab every year. The great literary importance of this legend is that it served as the model of Dante's immortal trilogy. The Sūfis have made the story a symbol of the soul's ascension from the world of the flesh to the world of mystic communion with God.

CHAPTER SIX

SECTS

(A) KHĀRIJITES

FROM early days Islam split up into a large number of sects, most of which are now obsolete; and, as would be expected the modern Muslim knows no more about them than the average Christian knows about the early heresies of the Church. Here we shall take into account only the most important sects which either exist to this day or have left a permanent mark on Islam. It may be noted in passing that there is a tendency among modern Muslims to look with a more indulgent eye on some of these vagaries, and to recognize that they may have a contribution to make to the development of modern Islam.

Generally speaking, it is difficult to separate the political and the theological differences which gave rise to some of these sects. Ash'arī, one of the early writers on heresies, says:

After the death of their Prophet men differed about many matters and resolved themselves into separate sects, though Islam embraced them all. The first difference which arose in Islam was in regard to the Imamate. When Allah took his Prophet to his Paradise the Helpers in Medina wanted to elect one of their own men, and when Abū Bakr heard of this he told them that the Imāmate must belong to one of the Quraysh, and when he told them that the Prophet had stated this they acknowledged the truth of it and gave their allegiance to him. . . . During his life-time, and that of his successor 'Umar, no further dispute arose, but when 'Uthmān succeeded dissension was so great that he was slain, and after his death people differed about him violently. The orthodox party said that he was a good man, and that those who had killed him were guilty of a serious crime. Others denied this, and the controversy has gone on to the present day. Similarly, when ʿAlī was elected, people differed; some opposed his headship, others stood aloof from the matter, while others upheld him, and this controversy has endured to the present day.

The first three Caliphs were all related to Muhammad by marriage. ʿAlī, the fourth, was the nearest in blood because he was his cousin and the husband of his daughter Fātima. ʿUthmān, the third Caliph, belonged to the family of the Umayyads who had been notorious for their opposition to the prophet before he came to power. When ʿUthmān was murdered, Muʿāwiya, the governor of Syria afterwards to become caliph, was the natural avenger of his blood, and when ʿAlī assumed the caliphate war broke out between them. ʿAlī was forced to agree to arbitration, and the decision of the umpires, which seems to have been prearranged, went against him.

Among ʿAlī's followers was a large group, the Khārijites (seceders), who regarded arbitration as an act of treason against God, the sole arbitrator. The judgement of God could be expected only through the free choice of the whole community. They maintained that anyone, even a Negro slave, could be elected as the head of the Muslim community if he possessed the necessary qualifications. Purity of life was the only test. They went on to assert that anyone guilty of grave sin was an unbeliever and an apostate, and it was therefore their duty to kill him. The character and religious standpoint of these people is best illustrated by their doctrine of ritual purity. Every Muslim had to perform the ceremonial washings before prayer. The Khārijites went much further and said that evil speaking, lying, and slander destroyed ritual purity and made men unfit for prayer. In accordance with their principles they withdrew from 'Alī and bitterly opposed Mu'āwiya. As upholders of the democratic principle they attracted many who were dissatisfied with the government for one reason or another. For instance, the Berbers found their doctrines agreeable in their revolt against the Umayyad governors. After the Khārijites had been suppressed in the various regions they continued to exist in scattered groups. It is interesting to observe the many points on which they agreed with the Mu'tazila.[1] Some of them went so far as to deny that the sūra of Joseph formed a part of the true Qurān; they said that it was a love story which had no place there. Some, too, asserted that God had left men free to believe or not to believe, that he did not create their actions, nor did he necessarily will that they should behave as they did. They were stern, uncompromising, and fanatical. They declared that those who refused to fight unjust rulers were infidels, and they utterly rejected dissimulation (taqīya) in word and deed. They held that those who persisted in a particular sin were infidels. Thus they were at liberty to kill all Muslims outside their own community.

Khārijites are found today in North Africa under the name of Ibādis or Abādis, in 'Uman and Zanzibar. They are a separate community outside the four orthodox schools, though on the whole the difference between them is not very great. In Algeria they keep very much to themselves. Marriage outside their sect is uncommon, so that their tenets and characteristics have been preserved. As one would expect of such a turbulent non-conforming sect, they split up into numerous parties in early days and lost the superficial unity which was based as much on negation as on positive principles. Perhaps

1. See page 129 f.

their greatest importance today lies in their undoubted influence on the Wahhābīs who are now in command of most of Arabia proper under the Saʿūdī dynasty, though, of course, those views which they shared with the Muʿtazila are strictly excluded.

(B) MURJI'ITES

This sect has long since passed away, but its influence on orthodox Islam has been great and lasting. Like so many of the sects, the Murji'-ites had a political origin. They were men who refused to take life too seriously. They refused to engage in strife against the Umayyad dynasty, arguing that they were in fact the rulers of the Muslim State, and that they were Muslims who believed in the unity of God and the apostleship of Muhammad. Therefore, they said, the good Muslim should hold aloof from the wars provoked by Shīʿa and Khārijites. The name Murji'ī means 'one who postpones' (judgement until the last day when the secrets of all hearts shall be revealed). In ʿAbbāsid times when the question of the caliphate was no longer so thorny they showed the same easygoing tolerance in the theological sphere. They did not look too closely at the sins of others: there was only one unforgivable sin, and that was polytheism. All that really mattered, they said, was faith. To them faith was an entity in itself: grievous sin could not impair it nor could good works increase it. They explicitly affirmed that fornication and theft would not debar a believer in the unity of God from Paradise.

The accepted doctrine of Islam, that one who commits mortal sins is not to be declared an infidel; that he remains a Muslim whatever he has done; that if he repents his repentance will be accepted by God; and if he does not abandon his sins he will be left to the merciful decision of God, owed much to the Murji'-ite opposition to the Khārijite thesis that mortal sin involves the punishment of hell. This is part of the extraordinary tolerance of Islam within its own boundaries. Provided that a man accepts the two fundamental assertions of Islam, the unity of God and the apostleship of Muhammad, any deviation from the right path is tolerated; though, it is only right to add, not approved. In any event the mortal sinner is guaranteed the prophet's intercession on the day of judgement.

(c) shī'a

As we have just seen, 'Alī, the fourth Caliph, could take an army into the field in support of his claims to the caliphate, and though by a trick he was theoretically deposed, he still remained a Caliph, and the orthodox community has always regarded him as the last of the four rightly guided Caliphs of Islam. In effect 'Alī was shorn of the most important areas which the earlier Muslims had conquered. Syria possessed the only strong military force, trained and, to some extent, disciplined by the Byzantines as frontier guards in their wars with Persia, and Mu'āwiya's rule there was unchallenged. He soon seized Egypt and raided Iraq as he pleased. The unfortunate 'Alī was murdered by the Khārijites in A.H. 661; his son Hasan resigned his claim to the Caliphate. Mu'āwiya was proclaimed Caliph at Jerusalem in the same year. His reign marked a vast expansion of the Arab empire. The Arabs captured Herāt, Kābul, and Bukhāra, advanced along the southern coast of the Mediterranean, defeated the Byzantines in a naval battle, and even attacked Constantinople itself. Hasan died a few years later. The Shī'a assert that he was poisoned at Mu'āwiya's instigation, and therefore was a martyr. His younger brother Husayn, who had lived quietly at Medina throughout Muʿāwiya's reign, came out in open rebellion against Yazīd, who had succeeded to the caliphate in 680, and set out for Kūfa at the invitation of the Iraqis. His force, consisting of a mere 200 men, was surrounded by vastly superior forces at Karbalā, and as they refused to surrender they were cut to pieces. The victor cut off the head of Husayn, the prophet's grandson, and sent it to Damascus. It was afterwards buried with his body in Karbalā, now one of the great sanctuaries of the Shīʿa. The tenth of Muharram, the day of the slaughter, marks the culmination of the ten days' lamentation which is observed every year by the Shīʿa. The great feature of this celebration is the Passion Play in Kāzimayn just outside Baghdād on the tenth day called ʿĀshūrā. This is followed forty days later by another Passion Play called 'The Return of the Head', which is enacted at Karbalā.

Politically ʿAlī's party appeared to be impotent, and their claim to the command of an empire which had been won largely by their rivals must have seemed extravagant, to say the least of it, to their contemporaries in Syria. Nevertheless they could count on the support of all those who for various reasons were dissatisfied with the ruling house. Although the movement was primarily Arab in origin, the vast bulk of these malcontents in the following generations was made up of the Mawālī, that is non-Arabs, who had accepted Islam and claimed exemption from the taxes and social disabilities to which non-Muslims were subject. The old Arab aristocracy, as we have seen, never fully admitted their claims. [This injustice was the more keenly felt because large numbers of these people had fought in the Arab armies for less pay and only such booty as they could snatch from the unwilling

Arabs. When it is remembered that these people were the heirs to the old Byzantine and Persian civilizations, and that they provided the bulk of the civil servants and learned professions, it is easy to see that all the material for a revolution lay at hand.]

What had begun as a political and social revolt soon acquired a religious character. A change of tactics was called for if the Muslim world was to be won over to their side. A man named Mukhtār headed a revolt in the name of Muhammad al-Hanafīya, the son of ʿAlī by a wife other than Fātima, and though he failed in his attempt his rising had an important sequel. He gave out that this Muhammad was not dead but had retired into concealment in the mountains around Mecca, and the faithful must expect his second coming to restore peace and justice to the world. Such was the birth of the Mahdī legend, which has given rise to countless pretenders down to modern times.

The Shīʿa now began to elaborate their specific doctrines. First of all, they rejected the principle of the consensus of the community, and substituted for it the doctrine that there was an infallible Imām in every age to whom alone God entrusted the guidance of his servants. Their propaganda met with great success in that it hastened the overthrow of the Umayyads. But once more they were tricked. Their victory brought the ʿAbbāsids to power, and their leaders were slain. Later the grave of Husayn was destroyed, and as many as possible of those who stood in the direct line of descent from ʿAlī were liquidated.

The Shīʿa taught that the faithful must believe in all the Imāms, and especially in the Imām of their own time. This belief was exalted into an additional 'pillar of Islam'. Among Sunnīs the Caliph is the head of the community, responsible for the administration of justice through the *sharī'a*, and for the defence of the realm of Islam, and he owes his office either to the choice of the community or to the nomination of his predecessor. Not so the Imām of the Shī'a. He is the divinely appointed ruler and teacher of the faithful who has succeeded to the prerogatives of the prophet himself. He possesses super-human qualities which descend to him from the first man, Adam, through Muhammad, a divine light which is given to chosen mortals from generation to generation. In popular beliefs which survive in some places to this day, the Imām's body throws no shadow and he cannot be physically harmed.

Among the extravagances of some of the Shī'a cults which still live on is the belief that 'Alī and the Imāms are incarna-tions of the Godhead, partakers of his attributes and powers, their bodies being but accidents inseparable from their visible forms. It is a strange and mysterious fact that sects whose very existence is a denial of the fundamental thesis of Islam should be tolerated within that community. However, it is only fair to add that they are not representative of the Shī'a as a whole. The latter hold that 'Alī is second to, or some-times equal to, Muhammad, but they do not go so far as to assert that it was he who should have received the divine message and not Muhammad.

Islam goes far beyond the Jewish and Christian veneration for prophets as men inspired by God to reveal his will to the world, in claiming that the prophets, and especially Muham-mad the seal of the prophets, were without sin and infallible. The Sunnīs differ among themselves as to the extent of this impeccability. Did it apply to all sin or only mortal sin? And could the prophets fall into the lesser sins of ordinary men? In the *Fiqh Akbar II*, which probably dates from the tenth century, we read:

All the Prophets are exempt from sins both light and grave, from unbelief and sordid deeds. Yet stumbling and mistakes may happen on their part. Muhammad is His Beloved, His Servant, His Apostle, His Prophet, His Chosen and Elect. He did not serve idols, nor was he at any time a polytheist even for a single moment, and he never committed a light or a grave sin.

This is now the accepted doctrine of Islam. Here two points may be made:

(1) There is a sharp break with canonical tradition which records that several of the prophets were guilty of grave sins, and early writers quote Muhammad as saying that in his youth he offered sacrifices to a heathen deity in Mecca. Furthermore, there is no trace of a doctrine of Muhammad's sinlessness in the canonical traditions.

(2) The doctrine is in flat contradiction of sūra 48:2, where it is said 'that God may forgive thee thy early and later sins.' And, we may add, to the whole spirit and tenor of Muhammad's words.

(3) The assertion of the doctrine would seem to be to some extent due to the necessity for providing a counterblast both to the Shī'a and to the Christians. If no claim was made on behalf of Muhammad, his case against the sinless Imām of the Shī'a, and the sinless Jesus of the Christians, would go by default. The high place which the latter holds in the Qurān and Muslim tradition would prevent them from assailing his claim to sinlessness even had they desired to do so. There is no trace of any such desire.

The outstanding difference between Sunnī and Shī'a doctrines of infallibility and superhuman knowledge is that with the former infallibility is not a quality inherent in the prophet by virtue of his being, but a special grace from God. His superhuman knowledge is given him from time to time by

God, whose message he repeats to men. His merit was to be chosen by God to be his mouthpiece. Thus the Sunnīs kept much closer to the qurānic texts like 47:66: 'Say; none in Heaven and earth knows what is hidden but God.' On the other hand, with the Shī'a sinlessness and infallibility are in the imāms and of them. They possess a secret knowledge inherited from their superhuman forbears by which they know all that will happen in the world until the Resurrection Day. Therefore they cannot err. They are the sole and ultimate authority in the interpretation of the Qurān, the source of all truth, and the only beings with the right to men's obedience. Therefore all doctrine must have their authority. As Goldziher has said:[1]

If we wish to state concisely the difference between Sunnī and Shī'a Islam we should say that the former is a Church founded on the consent of the community, the latter is an authoritarian Church.

This is true in theory, but in practice, as we have seen above, the differences do not radically affect the way of life in the two great divisions of the Muslim community.

The Shī'a very soon split up into a large number of sects. We can only look at those which have left a permanent mark on Islam. The most important of these is the 'Twelvers' or Imāmites, who form a large community to this day. They recognize twelve Imāms in the 'Alī-Fātima line which ends with Muhammad al-Mahdī. He disappeared from the world in 880 and is believed to be preserved against the day of his second coming as Mahdī (a word which means 'guided one'), the hidden Imām whom the faithful await to restore justice and righteousness to the world. All the various sects of the Shī'a have this hope in common. They differ in expecting a

1. *Vorlesungen über den Islam*, Heidelberg, 1910, p. 226.

different man to reappear. No doubt this doctrine of the second coming was largely influenced by Jewish and Christian Messianic hopes. But it is worth noticing that it seems to be almost a world-wide phenomenon, it being a belief held by some Indians, Mongolians, Peruvians, Chinese, and other nations. Through the centuries Mahdīs have appeared in various Muslim countries from time to time. The British army has gone into action against at least two in modern times, 'the Mad Mullah of Somaliland', and 'the Mahdī of the Sudan'. This belief has always been much stronger among the Shī'a than among the Sunnīs. Within the ranks of the former it is fundamental to their religion, and there is a large apocalyptic literature concerned with calculations as to when the Redeemer may be expected. In later Sunnī tradition the Mahdī is Jesus who will, when he returns to the earth, slay the anti-Christ. Ibn Khaldūn, one of the greatest thinkers that Islam has produced, says outright that the belief in the coming of a Mahdī is of popular origin. He knows no trustworthy authority for it. The strength of the idea among the Shī'a is due to their feeling that they are members of a body that has been deprived of its rights. 'Alī to them is the only true ruler of Islam's destinies, and as all their efforts to get this view accepted have failed, they have taken refuge in a Messianic restoration in an indefinite future.

The stronghold of the 'Twelvers' is Persia. There the Imāms are divine hypostases. Prayers with special formulas are reserved for them. Sunday is sacred to 'Alī and Fātima, the second hour of each day to Hasan, the third to Husayn, and so on. Pilgrimage to their tombs procures special rewards.[1]

Some groups of this sect are still to be met with in India,

1. Cl. Huart, *E.I.*, p. 564.

Iraq, and Syria. The position in Morocco is anomalous. The Sharīf and his subjects are Shī'as, but they live under the legal Sunnī School of Mālik. As would be expected from such a background, they show none of that intolerance towards Sunnīs which is expressed in Persia and Iraq.

Another branch which has survived to this day is the Zaydis, named after the fourth Imām, Zayd. In the third century of Islam they had spread far and wide, but now they are hardly found outside the Yaman. They are much the most broadminded of the Shī'a and differ from the bulk of them in refusing to tolerate *mut'a* marriages. They have their own law books.

An extraordinarily interesting offshoot of the Shī'as is the Ismā'īlīya, so named because in opposition to the rest of the Shī'as they regard Ismā'īl as the seventh Imām. Unfortunately we know very little about this man. To his followers he is, of course, second only to God himself, but Sunnīs and 'Twelvers' writers speak of him as an evil person who was deprived of his right to succeed to the Imāmate by his father Ja'far. Here we are concerned with what the Ismā'īlīya movement became rather than with the many historical problems that vex the historian. Ismā'īlism became, and has remained, a secret society. Those who know of it from within are initiates who dare not give a clear account of their beliefs. Such writings as the orientalist possesses, or has access to, conceal as much as they reveal. This much can be said, the movement had an enormous success; in the eleventh century of our era it had spread throughout the Muhammadan world from the Atlantic to India and threatened the future of Islam. Though it is shorn of all its former power it still can claim a large number of adherents.

One of the branches of this sect has added a word to our

vocabulary. The Assassins of the Middle Ages were the men drunk with hashīsh who went out to assassinate all those who had incurred their Master's anger. Their leader was known to the Crusaders as 'The Old Man of the Mountains'. From his impregnable fortress in Alamūt, 'the eagle's nest', north-west of Qazwīn, and from other strongholds in the Lebanon, the leader of the Assassins spread terror far and wide until they were all stamped out by the hordes of the Mongols in the thirteenth century. However, it must not be supposed that the Assassins and Qarmathians who sacked Mecca and carried off the Black Stone are typical of the Ismā'īlīs as a whole. Their philosophy is fundamentally neo-Platonic, and on an emanation basis they built a theory of a chain of mani-festations of the world intellect beginning with Adam, each adding to the instruction and achievements of his prede-cessor. This had the result of reducing Muhammad to an intermediate member of a series which had not run its course. He was not 'the seal of the prophets'. They taught that the law sacred to Muslims was not meant for the instructed, and its prohibitions were but mere allegories. Such were the opinions held by the orthodox about the Ismā'īlīs, and there is considerable truth in them. But it is only a part of the truth. The enormous success of their movement cannot have been due to the negation of the prevailing religion of their day, and one must look deeper for the causes of their early success. No doubt, like every other religious or social movement, Ismā'īlīsm was exploited by its leaders for their own ends, but that must not blind us to the appeal which it made to the masses. The teaching that laws had been invented to keep the lower orders quiet in the interests of their rulers found a ready response, and the leaders of Islam at the time recog-nized that the appeal which the movement had for the poorer classes made it a serious menace to the existing state of society. It differed from all other sects, and here it is like the Bahā'ī movement today in that it appealed to members of all religions – Muslims, Jews, Christians, Mandaeans, and others – and offered them a system in which it was claimed that all that was of real value in their respective religions was retained. Fanaticism was condemned and renounced, and the teaching of all religions was subsumed in the alleged greater truth of the Ismā'īlīs. However broadminded such an attitude would seem to be, one could hardly expect any member of the three great monotheistic religions of the world to welcome with enthusiasm the accession of a convert like 'Umar Khayyām, who is said to have been an Ismā'īlī. In essence Ismā'īlism is not a fanatical warlike form of sectarianism such as one might expect from its history in the Middle Ages. The Agha Khān, a descendant of the chief of the Assassins, once a President of the All India Muslim League, was a warm supporter of British rule in India before the advent of the new State of Pakistan.

An offshoot of the Ismā'īlīs exists today in the mountains of the Lebanon, the Anti-Lebanon, and Haurān, under the name of Druzes. They get their name from a man called Darazī, who proclaimed the divinity of the Fātimid Caliph in Cairo who had assumed the name of al-Hākim bi-Amri'llāh who disappeared in A.D. 1021. Whether he was murdered or whether he simply disappeared it is not possible to say. Darazī, according to some authorities, was forced to retire to Syria where he was slain. The ethnological origin of the Druzes is somewhat obscure. To them Hākim is still alive in concealment, and so their connexion with the Shī'a sects is obvious. A good many of their books are known, but the secrets of their community are well preserved. It is sometimes alleged that they have much in common with Free-masons, but if this is true it is impossible to get them to admit the fact. They certainly do not respond to any of the signs common among Masons, and such technical terms as are known do not indicate that there is any connexion whatever. The door of their secrets is close tiled. They are a friendly, industrious, and intelligent people, whom it is always a pleasure to meet. The history of their relations with their neighbours in the nineteenth century is anything but happy. They were responsible for three separate massacres of Christians; the last in 1860 brought about the active intervention of the French on behalf of the Christian population. Their connexion with Islam would seem to be little more than nominal.

(D) MUʿTAZILITES

The tenets of this party are discussed in the next chapter. They were not a sect in the strict sense of the word, but rather a group of thinkers who could count adherents in most of the sects proper. Perhaps the best term for them would be 'Modernists'. They rejected the traditional interpretation of the Qurān and the dogmas of the orthodox school, and claimed the right to judge revelation in the light of reason and the tenets of philosophy.

Arabic literature on the sects is enormous, as is the number of them. No good purpose would be served by discussing them here. They have gone the way of all such movements and have left little or no trace of their passing.

(E) AHMADĪYA

The Ahmadīya are the most recent sect in Islam. Their founder was a certain Mīrzā Ghulām Ahmad al Qādiānī who died in 1908. Before his death they had asked to be registered as a separate Muhammadan sect in India. They have been extraordinarily successful in propagating their tenets: they have gained thousands of converts in South-East Asia and Africa, and their claim that they now have a million adherents is probably not an exaggeration.

After the death of Ahmad's son, Kamāl al-Dīn and Muhammad 'Alī left the parent body and formed the Lahore party, leaving the original Ahmadīs with the title of Qādiānīs. The schism occurred on the vital question of the status of the founder Ahmad. To the Qādiānīs he was a prophet: to the seceders he was merely a reformer. The latter retain their original mosque at Woking: the former have a mosque in London itself.

The distinctive doctrines of the Qādiānīs are:

(1) No verse in the Qurān is, or can be, abrogated. If one verse appears to be inconsistent with another, that is due to faulty exegesis.

(2) *Jihād* or 'holy war' has lapsed, and coercion in religion is condemned.

(3) To say that Muhammad is the 'seal of the prophets' does not mean that he is the last of them. A seal is a 'hallmark' and he embodies the perfection of prophethood; but a prophet or apostle can come after him as did the Hebrew prophets after Moses.

(4) Jesus is dead like the rest of the prophets and he did not ascend bodily into heaven.

(5) Hell is not everlasting.

(6) Apostasy is not punishable by death.

(7) Any innovation in religious practice is culpable. The worship of saints is an invasion of the prerogative of God.

(8) *Ijmāʿ* or catholic consent (cf. p. 100) is generally limited to the prophet's Companions.

(9) Revelation will always remain a privilege of the true believer.

(10) Belief in Mīrzā Ghulām Ahmad al Qādiānī as the Messiah-Mahdī is an article of faith. Faith is incomplete without it.

(11) Spirituality in religion is more important than legalism. An Ahmadī need not belong to any particular *madhhab* or school of law.

(12) The mediaeval *ʿulamā* need not be followed in the interpretation of Qurān and *hadīth*.

Naturally articles 3, 4, and 10 are anathema to the orthodox Muslim and on more than one occasion numbers of Ahmadīs have been massacred. It will be a surprise to many to learn that the tomb of Jesus is to be seen at Srinagar. It is claimed that the evidence that it is his tomb is 'irrefutable'. So indeed it is, because it is non-existent!

CHAPTER SEVEN

PHILOSOPHY AND THE GENESIS
OF THE CREEDS

THE great centres of Greek learning in Syria, Egypt, Mesopotamia, and Persia were overrun by the Arabs within a few
years of Muhammad's death. Therefore it was inevitable that
the Muslims should become acquainted with the nature of
Greek thought and especially philosophy both from debates
and arguments with members of the old religions that were
frequent, and from the incorporation by way of conversion
of thousands who had lived under the old empires. Without
going into any detail we may note that as early as the seventh
century A.D. St John of Damascus argued with the 'Saracens'
about the meaning of the terms 'word' and 'spirit' applied
to Christ in the Qurān. Were they created or uncreate? What
was the origin of evil? Is it caused by God or by man? If God
commands a murderer to kill, then the murderer ought to
be praised for having fulfilled God's commandments. As we
shall see, these points were taken up with enthusiasm by one
school of thought among the Muslims and greatly influenced
the form that orthodox dogma was to assume.

After the triumphant entry of Greek philosophy into the
Arab world we must wait until the reign of Ma'mūn, the
Caliph in Baghdād who in the early ninth century ordered
that the chief books of Greek learning should be translated
into Arabic, for a full discussion of these problems. Philosophy, medicine, mathematics, astronomy, and the other
sciences known to the ancients were all made available to
educated Arabs. Syriac-speaking Christians did most of the

work. Plato, Aristotle, and the Neo-Platonists were now at everyone's disposal, and soon a school of Arab philosophers arose whose names were famous in Europe in the Middle Ages. Only one of them was an Arab by race, but as they all wrote in Arabic the Arabs are generally credited with their achievements.

Our concern is simply with philosophy as it affected the theology of the Muslim community, and here, of course, we must bear in mind that the average everyday Muslim whom one meets knows no more about the subject than does the average Englishman about the philosophical background of Christian theology. The language of the Athanasian Creed does its best for him, but without a knowledge of the underlying philosophical concepts he cannot grasp more than its general intention. Therefore in writing briefly of Muslim theology it seems best to ignore even such vitally important matters as the grafting of Neo-Platonism on to Aristotelianism through the unfortunate attribution to Aristotle of a Neo-Platonic work, and to concentrate on those matters which have given Islam the dogmatic character it holds to this day. The main points are: (a) the nature of God, (b) the nature of the Qurān, and (c) man's relation to God.

Historically these questions are associated with a school called the Mu'tazila, who succeeded to an earlier school known as the Qadarites who maintained that man had power to choose his acts. It must not be supposed that the Mu'tazila were a sect in the ordinary sense of the word; their adherents numbered men from Sunnī and Shī'a alike. Unhappily, however, their abuse of power made them and their views anathema to the orthodox, and after a brief reign as the dominant school of thought they were rigorously suppressed. Undoubtedly their intention was to provide a sound philosophical basis for Islam, and the name they gave themselves, 'the Champions of the Divine Justice and Unity', is a sufficient witness to the purity of their motives.

(*a*) Their fundamental tenet was the unity of God. They denied that God could be said to have any essential or eternal qualities. He could be described as Lord, Possessor, seeing, hearing, and so on, but not in the sense that Lordship, ownership, and sensual qualities were inherent in him. Eternity was the only attribute that could be ascribed to God. They argued that if these attributes which the orthodox had constructed from the names applied to God in the Qurān existed in the divine essence, that would constitute plurality in the Godhead and destroy the oneness of Allāh. They rejected all forms of anthropomorphism and offended the faithful by denying that God could be seen by the eyes of the believers in Heaven, and this in spite of the affirmation in the Qurān. And also in their absolute rejection of anthropomorphism they had to explain away texts which speak of God's hands, and eyes, and face, and the throne on which he sat. They opposed to these texts and the vulgar belief based on them the philosophical argument that God being infinite could not be in a place, for that would entail that he was finite. It might seem that as they accepted the fact that God knew and had power and could see, and so on, it was merely splitting words to say that he did not possess the qualities by which such powers could be exercised. But this is not so. By asserting that these qualities were inseparable from himself they prepared the way for their own doctrine.

(*b*) The nature of the Qurān. The idea of a heavenly tablet is as old as religion itself. It was familiar to the ancient heathendom of Mesopotamia, and Judaism in its traditional literature has crowned the Torah as pre-existent. In Christianity preexistence is ascribed to the Word, but the Logos, of course, has a different significance. But Muhammad taught that the Qurān was a transcript of the tablet preserved in Heaven. To the Mu'tazila this doctrine was a stumbling-block because it invaded the realm of God's oneness. They argued that if the tablet, i.e. the Qurān, was eternal and uncreate, it must be another God, for it was not God, and yet it was other than God, and in any case was an invasion of the true unitarian religion. It was here that the real sting in the Mu'tazila movement struck home. It would not matter vitally if men held that God willed not by will but by Himself, but it would matter if the Qurān, the speech of God, was a thing created in time. The Mu'tazila raised several difficulties for their opponents: how could the words which God is said to have addressed to Moses have been eternal and uncreate when Moses was a creature of time? Moreoever, the Qurān contains the speech of Moses and others. Then there was the further question, what was the relation of this hypothetical uncreate eternal Qurān to the copies read by Muslims and recited by their tongues? The answers to these questions are contained in the creed of Ash'arī, which will be dealt with later. The latter in itself is sufficient to show what influence the views and arguments of the Mu'tazila exercised on orthodox Islam. They compelled the theologians to think out their position and to provide answers to the many problems raised by a rationalistic interpretation of revelation.

(c) The Mu'tazila felt very keenly the moral difficulty inherent in the assertion that God misled sinners, decreed their evil deeds, and punished them in hell for the same. It may be noted that the Qurān is not consistent on this point. There are texts which clearly assert that man is responsible for his own actions, though the majority of texts seem to assert that they are definitely decreed. The Mu'tazila dealt with these passages as best they could by softening the language of predestination, but still it cannot be denied that the orthodox party had the Qurān on their side when they asserted that God's predestination was absolute. This view is borne out by the chapter on predestination in the books of canonical tradition which do not contain a single saying of Muhammad's which leaves freedom of action to man. Everything is predestined from the first and a man's fate is fixed before he is born. There are good reasons for believing that these traditions were forged at a time when the controversy was at its height, and their chief value lies in the way they illustrate how far the orthodox were prepared to go in defence of their tenets and the statements in the Qurān. However, they could arrive at their interpretation only by disregarding such plain statements as: 'The truth is from your Lord, let him who will believe and let him who will disbelieve.' (Sūra 18:28.) The Mu'tazila found the harsh doctrine of predestination to damnation intolerable. To them it was abhorrent that it should be thought that man would be punished for acts which God himself had commanded him to perform. It was their reaction against this doctrine and their assertion of the divine justice in its relation to man that led them to claim their title as Champions of the Divine Justice. God, they said, was worshipped as the Compassionate and Merciful, and it was unthinkable that he would not do his best for his creatures. They did not deny the all-embracing power of God, but they asserted that there was a difference between what God willed and what he commanded. It was altogether wrong to posit a relation between him and evil, and it was equally unthinkable that he would punish man for what he himself had commanded. Therefore man must be the author of his own good and evil deeds, his faith and his unbelief, and God gives him power to make his free unfettered choice. Nothing that man does that God has not commanded or that he has prohibited has been willed by God but by man himself.

So far it would appear that Mu'tazila theology was in a sense less harsh than the orthodox belief, but in another way it was much more severe. It gave man the privilege of full responsibility for his acts, but this responsibility was accompanied by its necessary consequences. If man committed mortal sins he was condemned to hell for ever with no prospect of escape, and no intercession by Muhammad was to be looked for.

Orthodox reaction to the doctrine of freewill took rather a strange form. The Mu'tazilites were dubbed dualists because it was said that by their assertion that man has 'power' over his actions they made him the 'creator' of his works and thus encroached on the almighty power of God, for there would be two creators of actions. The Mu'tazilites were also accused of blasphemy in that they made God subject to an external law by saying that he *must* do what was best for man. God, the absolute Monarch, could do what he liked, good or evil. Further, they undermined revelation by asserting that there was such a thing as intrinsic good or evil. Evil was evil in itself, not because God said so. God in revelation distinguishes between good and evil in accordance with the dictate of reason. We do not need revelation to tell us what is beautiful and what is ugly.

To descend to practical issues for a moment. It is obvious that a doctrine of predestination has great dangers to the life of an individual or a nation. It is natural, though not logical, to take up the position that inasmuch as everything is decreed it is idle for man to make any effort. Undoubtedly among the ignorant this has been a characteristic of the Muhammadan world for centuries. But those who adopt that attitude towards life are ignorant of the many exhortations to be up and doing in the service of God which the Qurān contains, and also ignorant of the teaching that God makes easy the path of those who trust him. But there is another side to this acceptance of the divine will. It sustains people in terrible hardships and gives them fortitude in adversity because they believe that their sufferings are sent by God. This is a belief which from a religious point of view is wholly admirable. Carried to excess it has obvious dangers. When a European reads the Qurān text, 'Place your reliance on God', on the windscreen of a motor-bus which is driven full speed round a hairpin bend with a precipice on the near side he is only too ready, if he is a religious man, to obey the injunction; but at the same time he wishes that the driver would exercise common prudence. But the attitude of the local population is characteristic of Islam, the religion of complete and absolute resignation to what is believed to be the will of Allāh.

We must now consider the orthodox reaction to these arguments and the crystallizing of their reaction in the creeds. The mention of creeds inevitably suggests to the English reader a formula familiar to every practising Christian, but it would be quite wrong to suppose that the ordinary Muslim knows any one of the principal creeds. However, they have a very real value as statements of belief even if they are not part of the ordinary Muslim's religious instruction. They contain the considered opinion of Islam, but they are not a concise statement of faith which the ordinary man carries about with him. His life, as we have seen, is governed by the *sharī'a* and the worship of the Mosque.

Passing over some early statements of belief, we may single out the creed known as *Fiqh Akbar II* as representative of Islam. It was compiled about A.D. 1000, and is based largely on the teaching of Ash'arī, the most prominent figure in the formative period of Islamic theology. It consists of twenty-nine articles. All that can be given of it here is a summary of the more important of them. Allāh is absolute in his decrees of good and evil. He does not resemble his creatures in any respect. He has existed from eternity with his qualities, those belonging to his essence and those pertaining to his activity. The Qurān is the speech of Allāh written in books, preserved in memories, recited by tongues, revealed to the prophet. Whatever God quotes in the Qurān from Moses or others is his speech in relation to theirs. The speech of God is uncreate, but the speech of Moses and others is created. We speak with organs of speech and letters; God speaks without instruments and letters. With regard to anthropomorphism the creed goes on to assert that God has face, hand, and soul, but it is not legitimate to enquire how, for these belong to his qualities; God has no body. The doctrine of predestination is tempered, so far as the preserved tablet is concerned, by saying that its writing is of a descriptive, not a decisive, nature. Similarly, the doctrine of predestination is stated in terms which remove a good deal of the earlier crudities. God created men free from unbelief and from belief, then he gave them commandments and some disbelieved. Their denial was caused by God's abandoning them. He does not compel any of his creatures to believe or not to believe. All man's acts are his own acquisition, but God creates them, and they are caused by his will. With regard to a mortal sinner, it is said that he is not called an infidel or excluded from the faith. It is not denied that he may go to Hell, nor is it affirmed that he will remain there everlastingly, but it is affirmed that an unrepentant sinner must be left to the will of God. He may punish him in hell or he may forgive him. The intercession of the prophet on behalf of the faithful who have committed grave sins and deserve punishment is an article of faith. With regard to the beatific vision, it is said that the faithful will see God in Paradise with their bodily eyes, and there will be no distance between them and their Creator. All the verses of the Qurān are the speech of God and are equal in excellence and greatness. Some, however, are pre-eminent either in re-citation or in content. For example, the Throne verse (p. 75), because it deals with the majesty of God. Others possess ex-cellence only in regard to recitation, such as a description of the infidels. The ascension of the prophet is a fact, and whoso rejects it is a schismatic. The appearance of the Anti-Christ, the descent of Jesus from Heaven, as well as the other eschato-logical signs described in authentic tradition, will surely take place.

Dislike and open hostility to philosophy had long been widespread when al-Ghazzālī opened his attack on the philosophers in a book called *Tahāfut al-Falāsifa* (*The Inco-herence of the Philosophers*). This book had an enormous vogue in the Middle Ages, both in Arabic and in its Latin transla-tions. It is a special study which serves as a sort of appendix to his great work, *The Revival of the Religious Sciences* (see p. 148). In it he began by saying that the decay of faith in Islam was due to the respect which people showed for Socrates, Hippocrates, Plato, Aristotle, and others, and that he intended to explain the failures and incoherence of their arguments. Thus Aristotle contradicted Plato. But if their system of philosophy was as sound as their mathematics there would have been no need for any contradiction. Moreover, the Arab translators had given faulty translations of the original. The twenty chapters of his attack on the philosophers are named:

(1) The vanity of their assertion that the world had no beginning.
(2) And that it will have no end.
(3) An exposition of their subterfuge in asserting that God is the Maker of the world and that the world is his work.
(4) Their inability to prove that it had a Maker.
(5) Their inability to prove that there cannot be two Gods.
(6) The vanity of their denial of the Divine attributes.
(7) The vanity of their assertion that the first Being is not divided into genus and species.
(8) The vanity of their assertion that the first Being is simple without quiddity.
(9) Their inability to show that the first Being is incorporeal.
(10) Their inability to prove that the world has a maker and a cause.
(11) Their inability to show that the first Being knows aught but himself.
(12) Their inability to show that he knows his own essence.
(13) The vanity of their assertion that the first Being does not know particulars.
(14) Their assertion that Heaven is an animal moving in a circle in obedience to God.
(15) The vanity of what they say about the end that moves the sky.
(16) The vanity of their assertion that the souls of the heavens know all particulars.

(17) The vanity of their assertion that it is impossible that the accustomed order of things (i.e. natural law) should be ruptured.

(18) Their assertion that man's soul is a self-subsistent substance without body or accident.

(19) Their assertion of the impossibility of the annihilation of human souls.

(20) The vanity of their denial of the bodily resurrection to bliss or torment in Heaven or Hell with corporeal pleasures and pains.

This book provoked a retort which marks the climax of Arabian philosophy. After it nothing creative was written, and writers have simply repeated, epitomized, and commented on the books of their predecessors. This retort came from Spain, from the pen of one famous in the West under the name of Averroes (Ibn Rushd, d. A.D. 1198). He called his book *The Incoherence of the Incoherence*, and in it he goes through Ghazzālī's points one by one, and on the whole answers them decisively. It would take a disproportionate amount of time to examine this reply in detail, and we must reluctantly forgo the attempt. Modern science would seem to have proved that those of the pre-Aristotelian philosophers who held that the world came into being from some primitive matter were in the right. Aristotle himself affirmed that the universe always had been. Ghazzālī gives more space to this question than to any other theme. The philosophers argued that if the world had been created in time, something must have provided an initial impulse when it came out of non-existence or potential existence into actuality, and that that determinant must itself have had a determinant, and so on *ad infinitum*. Therefore, either the world has always been, or we must suppose that an eternal God took a decision in time, and this would involve a change within the changeless God which was unthinkable. Dr Van den Bergh has recently shown that Ghazzālī's reply, which is also that of St Thomas Aquinas, is taken from Philoponus, who said that a distinction must be made between God's eternal will and the eternity of the object of his will, or, as St Thomas puts it: 'From eternity God willed that the world should be, but He did not will that it should be from eternity.'

Averroes replied that the difficulty could not be disposed of so easily. If time entered into the divine decision, that is to say if any phenomenon was not eternal, its creation must have been willed at a given time. Therefore there must have been a new will in God, whether it is thrust back into eternity or not. And it is this novelty which cannot be admitted. But he goes on to say that the whole controversy has arisen through failure to see that the assumption that the divine will is like the human will is false. The God who needs nothing cannot will in the human sense of the word, and the world is and must be a natural emanation from him.

Infinity is a conception which men have always boggled at. Ghazzālī (and Shahrastānī, and others also for that matter) argued – and here he is again borrowing from Philoponus – that if the world had not begun in time, how can you account for your power to imagine that an infinite series has ended? Opinions will differ, but it seems to the writer that Averroes was right when he said that there never is an end of time within eternity, and you can never say that an infinite time is ended.

To Aristotle there was no absolute beginning, because everything becomes out of something else, and his thought in this respect is somewhat akin to modern theories of evolution. Now if becoming is nothing but the actual realization of potentiality, what is potentiality? Is it something, or is it not? This question had already been attacked by the Eleatics, who argued that there was no such thing as potentiality in nature. For example, death would remove a potential genius. Things either were or they were not. Ghazzālī adopts this argument of the Megarics not only because it suited his standpoint, but also because it fitted in to his attitude towards the law of cause. To a man who believes that fire does not burn wood because it is its nature so to do, and that it always will burn wood, there would be no difficulty in defining potentiality, which was but a hypothetical induction.

We have seen that the doctrine of miracles was bound up with this denial of causal law, and in view of the parallel movement of thought among the British sceptical school of philosophers whose most intransigent representative was Hume, we cannot deny the Muslim theologians' right to their theory of divine action from moment to moment as an explanation of what most rational people suppose to be cause and effect. To all these the answer of Averroes would be relevant. Every universal concept implies that the thinker knows the nature of things. When we tell a man to get wood we know and he knows what is meant, and we know and he knows that wood will burn. 'He who does away with causal law does away with mind itself.'

The Ash'arite school had tried to deal with the objection that man acts as though he knows that there is a nature in things, so that wood burns and water makes wet, by saying that God acts according to an established order so that man may have some guide as to how to adapt himself to the conditions of the world. When he imagines that he himself is writing it is because God has given him by way of acquisition the capacity to act in accordance with his decree. God creates his will from moment to moment, then the capacity to write, then the movement of the hand, and then the motion of the pen. As Macdonald has said: 'Man is thus a cinematographic automaton with the belief added that he is doing it all himself.' A thirteenth-century creed says: 'It is the nature of fire to burn according to those who hold the doctrine of nature, God curse them, but in reality God creates inflammability in the wood when it comes into contact with fire.'

Towards the end of the fifteenth century Sanūsī, an author who still has great influence in North Africa, wrote in his *Introduction to Theology:*

Some believe that causes are eternal and by their nature, i.e. their essence, exercise an independent effect without any act of God. This is the doctrine of many philosophers and naturalists, and many have asserted that the consensus of Muslims brands them as infidels. Others believe that they are temporal and exercise an effect on the objects with which they come into contact, not by their nature but by the power which God creates in them. Were He to take away that power their effect would cease. Such men are innovators, impious, and led astray. Whether or not they are infidels is disputed. Others believe that causes are temporal and exercise no effect on the objects with which they come into contact, either by their nature or by the power which is created in them, but they believe that they are inseparably connected with that with which they come into contact and cannot be dissociated from it. This is a belief that leads to infidelity, because it involves the denial of the miracles of the Prophets and what they have reported about death, the grave, and the next life, because all these things are ruptures of the ordinary cause of nature, wherein ordinary causes do not have their accustomed effects. Others believe that customary causes are temporal and have no effect on that with which they come into contact, either by their nature or by a power which is created in them, and that God has created them as signs and indications of the things which He wishes to create without any logical

CHAPTER EIGHT

MYSTICISM

THEOLOGY is a discipline which the ordinary layman in all religions is only too glad to leave to the professional theologians. The niceties of dogma, the codification of the articles of the creed, the definitions which repel as often as they satisfy, frequently drive men to quench their thirst for God in ecstatic experience rather than in intellectual search. Islam is no exception. Its greatest theologian, as we shall see, became disgusted with the subject of theology and philosophy and found peace in the mystic Path, though, be it noted, he never lost hold, at any rate in his writings, of the intellectual basis on which his early faith had been established. In the Qurān, despite its preoccupation with battles, spoils, and women, and the heavenly orchard with large-eyed houris and handsome boys, there is a strong note of other-worldliness and, to a lesser degree, of mysticism. The beautiful Throne verse has already been cited (page 75), and there are two other texts which have inspired Muslim mystics on countless occasions, namely, 'We are nearer to him [i.e. man] than the vein of his neck' and 'Wherever ye turn there is the face of God.' In the hearts of men longing for a deep and intimate knowledge of God, discussions of anthropomorphism and pantheism found no place. They concentrated on the text, 'A people whom He loveth and who love Him' (5:59). It was this text above all others which appealed to the Sūfīs, who sought to lose themselves in the divine love. Sūfī (from *sūf*, wool) was the nickname given to them by their countrymen because the early ascetics wore a garment of undyed wool like Christian ascetics.

There was a strong note of asceticism among the more serious of the early Muslims, who were disgusted at the widespread luxury and loose living which marked the Caliphates of Damascus and Baghdād. They enjoined austerity and prayer and gave themselves up to a life of contemplation and religious exercise. To what extent they were influenced by factors and forces outside Islam is of no moment. What is certain is that Islam itself with its doctrine, fasting, and litanies (*dhikr*), provided the authoritative background of their lives. These people were the non-militant counterparts of the puritan Khārijites who translated their disgust with worldliness into violent action. Ibrāhīm ibn Adham, prince of Balkh, whose conversion from a life of luxury and ease was brought about by a heavenly voice, is reported to have said of a man who was studying grammar: 'It would be better for him if he studied silence.' There is a simple restraint in the story of this man's call; his endeavour to evade it, his wholehearted response; and finally his life of utter poverty in devotion to God. While the Sūfīs could have such leaders they could not fail to attract the most devout men of their time.

Before the second century had ended the Sūfīs had already worked out a method of attaining the *gnosis* or mystic knowledge of God. Doubtless this method was the result of experience and observation. The Path by which their sects and leaders had ascended to an ecstatic union with God was the one that their followers must pursue. To give a detailed account of the stages in this Path, its 'stations' and its 'states', would introduce a note of mechanical formalism into a sublime subject which deserves more respectful treatment.

Suffice it to say that the preliminary stages were those familiar to students of Western mystical literature in the *via purgativa*. The language of Muhammadan mystics is much more daring than we are accustomed to expect. To many it would seem blasphemy, and, as we shall see, one of the most attractive characters among them was crucified on that account. A Persian used to cry 'Glory to me' during his ecstasies and claimed to have ascended to Heaven in a dream. This same man taught that the gnostic's essence is annihilated by a divine essence in which all trace of self is lost. To say 'I' and 'God' is to deny the unity of God. . . . Lover, beloved, and love are one. A mystic who combined mystical intuition with a firmer grasp of theology was Junayd (d. A.H. 298). Taking his stand on the Qurān, he said, much as St Augustine did in a Christian context, that the struggle of man in this world was to fulfil the covenant between man and God referred to in the Qurān, so that man could return to his primeval state. Thus he taught that though man died to himself he did not cease to exist as an individual, but his individuality or personality becomes perfect through God and in God. The love which the mystic feels for God is joy mingled with suffering in that he is separated from God as soon as the mystical experience is over, and he awaits the renewal of union with God when he is once more absent from the transitory world. His pupil Hallāj was so carried away by his ecstatic experience that he did not feel the dual nature of man, that is to say, his existence here as a single creature and his rapture in mystical communion with the Divine. He taught that man was God incarnate, and he looked to Jesus rather than to Muhammad as the supreme example of glorified humanity. God is love, and in his love he created man after his own image so that man might find that image within himself and attain to union with the divine nature. He used the term *hulūl*, meaning in-dwelling, a word which is associated in Muslim literature with the Christian doctrine of the incarnation. He did not go further than many of the Sūfīs in claiming that mystics are superior to prophets, revealing within themselves the creative truth which called them into being. His most heinous offence in the eyes of the orthodox was his claim *ana'l-haqq* (i.e. 'I am the truth'). He was well aware of the risk he was taking. He was condemned to death, and as he was led forth to be crucified and saw the cross and the nails he prayed for the bystanders in words that inevitably recall one of the sayings of Jesus on the cross: 'Father, forgive them, for they know not what they do.' His prayer ended with the words:

And these Thy servants who are gathered to slay me in zeal for Thy religion and in desire to win Thy favour, forgive them, O Lord, and have mercy upon them; for verily if Thou hadst revealed to them that which Thou has revealed to me, they would not have done what they have done; and if Thou hadst hidden from me that which Thou hast hidden from them, I should not have suffered this tribulation. Glory unto Thee in whatsoever Thou doest, and glory unto Thee in whatsoever Thou willest.

The depth and intensity of his feeling is beautifully brought out in the verses in which he tries to express the feeling of complete harmony with God which he enjoys:

> I am he whom I love, and he whom I love is I,
> We are two spirits dwelling in one body.
> If thou seest me, thou seest Him,
> And if thou seest Him, thou seest us both.

Hallāj was executed in A.D. 922, and from that time onwards, not unnaturally, the Sūfīs became more reticent in their public utterances, and their ecstatic experiences became the secrets of their order rather than the subject of their public addresses. Their language becomes veiled and allusive, the metaphors of love and wine recur again and again, and only those who held the key to their secrets could fully grasp the inner meaning of their verses. The scandal of Hallāj brought the Sūfīs as a whole under suspicion, and it must be admitted that the orthodox had much ground for complaint. One of the Persian mystics, Abū Saʿīd (d. A.D. 1049), regarded the *sharīʿa* as superfluous to those who had attained the goal of the mystic Path. He would not allow his disciples to go on pilgrimage to Mecca, and is said to have forbidden the dervishes to interrupt their dancing when the *muezzin* called to prayer. Here there is a clear departure for the practices of the early Sūfīs, who faithfully observed the *sunna* in these matters.

Passing over the many books that were written to explain the mystics' faith, and to show that Sūfīism was true in spirit and in form to orthodox faith and practice, we come to a man who established the right of Sūfīs to a place in the heart of the citadel of orthodoxy. This man was Abū Hāmid al-Ghazzālī, known to the west as Algazel, who was born in Tūs in A.D. 1059 (died in 1111). This man is one of the greatest figures in the religion of Islam. He had distinguished himself in all the philosophical, legal, and other studies of his time. He was Professor at the Nizāmīya Madrasa in Baghdād and was recognized as the greatest contemporary authority on theology and law. He himself could find no spiritual satisfaction in either. Convinced that God could not be found by speculation and study, he was thrown into such anguish of spirit that he abandoned his professorship and went about in search of truth. He sought it in vain among all the theological schools of his time. The theologians were useless, the

Imāmites with their infallible Imām were no better, and then he turned towards the mystics. His autobiography has often been compared to the *Confessions* of St Augustine. In it he tells us that he found that the mystic Path involved abandoning the delights of the flesh and getting rid of all evil thoughts and desires so that the mind could be cleared of everything but the thought of God. The way was to practise *dhikr*, that is the commemoration of God and the concentration of the mind upon him. He read the books of the Sūfīs and absorbed what he could, but he perceived that the real secret of the mystic cannot be learnt. It must be experienced in ecstasy and transformation of the self. Everything that he did seemed useless and pointless, even his work as a teacher. He was in the world and of the world, and his work had been but a means of self-glorification, not an undertaking for God's glory. He cast himself upon God, and God enabled him to abandon social eminence and prosperity, wife, children, and friends, and he left Baghdād. His great work, *The Revival of the Religious Sciences*, and his smaller but very important mystic work, *The Niche of the Lights*, contain the fruit of his life's labours. The former is divided into four parts; it is a comprehensive statement of dogmatic, moral, ascetic, and illuminative theology, and has no rival in the theological literature of Islam. It contains the whole duty of man in belief and practice, and as he sets it forth it is permeated by a spirit of ascetic and mystical devotion to God. 'To a large extent he succeeded in making orthodoxy mystical; it was impossible in the nature of things that equal success should attend his efforts to make mysticism orthodox.'[1]

In the smaller book which is intended for Sūfīs his language is often mysterious to a degree, and when the reader is led to

1. R. A. Nicholson in *The Legacy of Islam*, p. 222.

the door of the mystic's inner experience he often finds it closed with the remark that here is a mystery which the author is not at liberty to disclose. One cannot but suspect that Ghazzālī had reached the same point as Hallāj.

But there was another side to Sūfiism. Whether it had been concealed for centuries running parallel with the Neo-Platonic theories of the philosophers of the Shī'ī theologians, we do not know; but in the twelfth and thirteenth centuries a doctrine of the 'idea of Muhammad' appeared in Sūfi writings. There is a section in Ghazzālī's *Niche of the Lights* which might seem to point in the same direction, but there is nothing so downright as the Logos doctrine of Ibn 'Arabī, the Spaniard (1165–1240). The idea or reality of Muhammad, he says, is the creative, animating, and rational principle of the universe, the first intellect; he is the reality of realities whose manifestation is in the perfect man. Every prophet is a Logos whose individual Logoi are united in the idea of Muhammad. The perfect man is he in whom all the attributes of the macrocosm are reflected. The reality of Muhammad is the creative principle of the universe, and the perfect man is its cause.

This writer is extremely difficult to understand. His style is enigmatical, and his subject abstruse, and any translation must be largely an interpretation rather than a rendering of what the author wrote. It seems that he regarded himself as the seal of the saints, while admitting that Muhammad was the seal of the prophets. We can see in some of the utterances of his school a deep longing for a closer relation with the transcendent God of Islam. It is largely this that gives them the appearance of borrowing from Christian sources. Mystically they put forward the perfect man as the visible aspect of God in relation to the world. But in speaking of 'our Lord

Muhammad, the source of all mysteries and the cause of all phenomena', they did the prophet a great injustice. None could accuse him of making himself equal to God.

To the fascinating studies of the late Professor Asin of Madrid we owe the discovery of the enormous influence of Ibn 'Arabī on Dante. The Arab first described the infernal region, the heavens of the astronomers, the Paradise of the blessed, the choirs of angels round the divine light, and the beautiful woman who was his guide. Curiously enough, both Arab and Florentine were forced to write a commentary on their first works to show that their love-songs had an esoteric and not an amatory significance. The link between the two writers has since been discovered, and the fact of affiliation has now passed into the history of European literature. The significant point is that the narrative is based on the legend of Muhammad's ascent to Paradise.

From early days the Sūfīs recognized the necessity for a spiritual director to whom the novice owed blind obedience. He must no longer exercise his own judgement, but must be completely at the disposal of his *shaykh* or *pir*. Such a state of affairs could be possible only in an organized association, and all over the Muslim world men renowned for their spiritual gifts were surrounded by scores of eager pupils. The members of the organization were known as *faqīrs* or *darwīshes* poor men or beggars. A solemn rite of initiation awaited a novice, and after that he remained with his *shaykh* until he graduated as a leader. The community was housed in buildings endowed by supporters, and there the dervishes could give themselves up to their life of devotion, meditation, and various physical exercises. From the twelfth century onwards these orders spread all over the Muslim world. There were a large number of different orders held together by a common aim of losing self in God, but vastly different in ritual and in their attitude to Islamic orthodoxy. As in the monastic orders in Christendom there were countless lay brothers who met to practise *dhikr* and afterwards returned to their normal occupations in the outside world.

An extraordinary feature in some of the leaders was their religious indifference; for instance, Ibn 'Arabī could say that his heart was a temple for idols, a Ka'ba for pilgrims, the tablet of the Pentateuch and the Qurān; love alone was his religion. One of his pupils said that the Qurān is polytheism (*shirk*). The confession of the divine unity lay only in the speech of the Sūfīs. How deeply this thought of the all-embracing unity of the mystical approach to God was rooted among the Sūfīs can be seen from the lines of one of Avicenna's friends written some two centuries earlier:

> So long as mosque and school still stand
> The dervish work lies still to hand.
> While faith and unfaith stand apart
> There is no Muslim true of heart.

It would be impossible to give an account of all the dervish orders,[1] and only a few of the principal fraternities can be mentioned. One of the most attractive of these is the Qādirīya, named after 'Abd al-Qādir al-Jīlānī (d. A.D. 1166). He was a powerful preacher who is said to have converted many criminals in Baghdād and organized relief for the poor and needy. His biographers assert that he performed miracles from time to time. A volume of his sermons has been published. They show a noble, religious, and philanthropic spirit. In one of them he wishes that the gates of Hell could be shut, and that the gates of Heaven could be opened to all

1. See J. P. Brown, *The Darwishes or Oriental Spiritualism*, Oxford, 1927, a reprint of the original edition of 1867 with notes by H. A. Rose.

mankind. Undoubtedly he had great hypnotic powers, and an immense number of people flocked to hear him preach. A *ribāt* or monastery was built for him outside the city. The head of the Qādirī order who is in charge of his tomb today is said to be one of his direct descendants. The Qādirīs have remained true to the example of their founder in that they are tolerant, pious, and peace-loving men. They gave birth to a great many offshoots. The Rifā'īya, founded by Jīlānī's nephew, is notorious for its fanaticism and those practices which are associated with dervishes in the popular European mind, such as fire-walking, eating glass, handling snakes, and so on.

In North Africa, still a stronghold of Sūfiism, Marabouts enjoy great prestige. Their holy men are credited with magical powers, and their tombs are venerated and visited by thousands. In Turkey a series of edicts has greatly reduced the once enormous multitude of dervishes, and naturally their influence has declined. In India, as would be suspected, the dervish orders are permeated with Hindu influences, so that even the caste system has found place among them.

Something must now be said about dervish ritual and practice. Among the Naqshabandī order the *shaykh* recites the declaration of belief in Allāh and his prophet while the novice keeps his attention fixed by placing his heart opposite that of the *shaykh*. He shuts his eyes and his mouth, pressing his tongue against the roof of his mouth, and clenches his teeth and holds his breath. Then with great force he recites with his heart, but not with his tongue, the words of the *shaykh*. He must hold his breath so that within one respiration he can say the *dhikr* three times and so allow his heart to be impressed. Many travellers have described the dances and extravagances of the dervishes. Perhaps the best account is that given by Lane in his *Modern Egyptians*: he describes a great ring of devotees jumping and leaping into the air to the beat of tambourines, dancing wildly with no ordered movement until they are utterly exhausted. Lane saw one of them rush from the dance and put pieces of red-hot charcoal one after another into his mouth, chewing them and finally swallowing them; while another put a live coal into his mouth and inhaled until it was almost white-hot. As he let out his breath sparks flew out of his mouth. Lane says that though he watched them carefully he could not see any indication of pain on their faces. It used to be the practice in Cairo for the *shaykh* of one of the dervish orders to ride over the bodies of a number of followers who threw themselves in his path.

A more recent writer[1] gives an account of a dervish *dhikr* in Cairo just before the first world war. It took place in a long room with benches on either side. In the middle was a carpeted space with a railing in the form of a horseshoe. The Shaykh took his place at the open end of the horseshoe with his back towards the wall. The dervishes, men who had just come in from the street, stood inside the railing. The *shaykh* knelt sitting back on his heels and repeated the first chapter of the Qurān. Then the devotees recited the confession of faith and other phrases, accompanied by gestures of head and body, with great attention to breathing. Gradually the recitation and movements grew faster, the breathing being so regulated that the utterances of the formula produced a strong emotional effect. The writer noticed that the effect on some was a pleasant hypnosis, and he says that he himself was strongly tempted to join in the movements. There was none of that disorderly outburst of shrieking and leaping which

1. D. B. Macdonald, *Aspects of Islam*, New York, 1911.

accompanied the celebrations attended by Lane. This writer mentions the regret which a converted Muslim felt at having to abandon these religious exercises. It is interesting to note that this particular man said that as a dervish he had developed unusual telepathic power, so that he knew what was going on at a distance and could even hear words that were spoken there. Claims to such powers are commonplace in Sūfī literature. Certainly stories one has heard from people of unimpeachable veracity confirm the existence of very remarkable powers, whatever the explanation of them may be.

However, these are but by-products of an unselfish mystical search for God which can be found in all religions worthy of the name. To Islam belongs the honour of having the richest and most variegated literature on this sublime subject.

To the question whether personality survives in the ultimate union with God the majority of Sūfīs would say that it does not. Despite the mystical union expressed in terms of love and marriage, the union with the world soul is the utmost imaginable bliss for mankind, and the Sūfī has a positive passion for losing himself in the infinity of the Godhead.

> Oh, let me not exist! for non-existence
> Proclaims in organ tones, 'To Him we shall return.'

CHAPTER NINE

ISLAM TODAY

NOTHING can be more misleading than a number of general statements based on imperfect and incomplete knowledge, and no man living has a thorough acquaintance with the millions of Muslims in Asia and Africa, to say nothing of scattered communities elsewhere, so that he can make authoritative pronouncements on Islam as a whole. All that can be done is to take into account what modern Muslims have written about their religion and so supplement it by what one has seen and heard. The result will be illuminating, but it will leave vast areas dark. Where little or nothing is written, and the people are inarticulate, nothing of real value can be said.

The question of overriding importance is: To what extent are modern Muslims affected by modern historical criticism, modern philosophy, and modern science? The answer must be that only those who have been students at universities with a Western tradition have any real understanding of these things, and they are a small, but by no means negligible, minority. In conversation many of them will take an un-orthodox view of the Qurān and a highly critical view of tradition, and some, as will be seen, have written fearlessly on the latter. But to treat the Qurān as the writing of a man, even of an inspired man, is more than they dare attempt: the power of the 'ulamā is too much for them, and no position in the public service would be open, or would remain open, to them if they expressed doubts about the Qurān being liter-ally the Word of God. In Egypt there is the example of the scholar and statesman Ṭāhā Ḥusayn. In one of his books he questioned whether Abraham and Ishmael had ever been in Mecca, and for this he was dismissed from his office in the University, in spite of his eminence as a scholar and his international reputation. A good many years passed before he was reinstated in public office. If such things could happen to a scholar whose patriotism and zeal for his country's progress were recognized by thousands of his countrymen, what hopes have lesser men of following the dictates of reason and conscience?

Recently a lecturer at al-Azhar, the famous university in Cairo which devotes itself to the study of traditional Islamic learning in all its aspects, published an article in which he denied that the law that ordered fasting throughout the month of Ramaḍān was binding on devout Muslims. Now fasting is one of the 'Pillars of Islam' and is prescribed in the Qurān (2:181). Not unnaturally protests against the writer's heresy came from many parts of the Muslim world. The offender was summoned to attend a disciplinary council by the Rector of al-Azhar who was supported by the ʿulamā elsewhere. Some of those who thought that the lecturer had gone too far admired his courage and deplored the action of the Rector. In one journal an editor wrote: 'We want al-Azhar to be a citadel of free thinking, not a cemetery for freedom of thought, or a stronghold of ignorance and reaction.' These words were enthusiastically acclaimed in Cairo and the old-fashioned curriculum and methods of instruction at al-Azhar were severely criticized. However, the public were denied the *cause célèbre* that they hoped for because, before the tribunal sat, the shaykh retracted what he had written and confessed that he had been mistaken.

In almost every Eastern capital today one can see the aeroplane overhead and the motor-car on the streets while, heedless of both, the camel walks slowly and superciliously along the public way, utterly indifferent to the traffic he dislocates and finally brings to a halt. Similarly in matters of the mind and spirit progressive characters may adopt modern ways of thought and make great use of them, but the old conservative who rules the masses goes on repeating word for word the teaching of his forefathers. In 1917 I saw the students at al-Azhar being taught geography from maps based ultimately on the old classical geographers; in 1950 I heard a lesson on grammar in the same mosque which took the form of learning by heart a medieval handbook on Arabic, regardless of the fact that comparative Semitic studies have made all earlier attempts to describe the genius of the Arabic language sterile and defective and at times positively misleading. The theory is wrong and the conclusions foredoomed to futility.

A reformer, whether in secular or religious matters – and there is no clear line between them – has thus to reckon with the enormous power of tradition and the dead weight of inertia. The question is not merely one of scholarship: it is economic also. If a new method of studying a subject is adopted, the teachers of the old way are no longer wanted by the rising generation. They must make way for those who know the new learning. It is not surprising that enormous opposition is encountered by those who would bring new life into the old organism. What would become of the host of 'ulamā, the muftīs, and the qāḍīs and so on, were it once admitted that the sharī'a was an invention of the centuries after Muhammad's death and that his revered name was falsely invoked to validate it? Obviously a class of men who had dominated their fellow-countrymen for centuries would go into retirement or have to find some other employment; and quite apart from the possibility that many of them are honestly convinced of the sanctity of their calling and of their credentials, how could they be expected to go through a course of study in what after all is Western criticism of an Eastern religion and an Eastern way of life? For us the problem is an old one; it was faced by Europe at the Reformation and the Renaissance, and it may well be that Islam is now at the threshold of a Reformation; however many of those who see that some reform is called for point ominously at the schism within the body of Christianity which resulted.

The attack on the authenticity of tradition on which the Muslim's life is based, began more than a thousand years ago, has once more come to the fore. Of course much has already gone by the board: the wearing of European dress, itself a violation of the *shari'a*, and the dropping of the old laws of almsgiving, pilgrimage, and so on by all but a minority, are among the most obvious changes which modern life has brought about. Nevertheless the old spirit is not dead: a student of mine was once rebuked by an imām for wearing a gold signet ring, because there was a tradition attributed to the prophet which forbade it. It had been given him by his father and he refused to abandon it. This is but a straw in the wind. Today great changes are taking place in the Muslim world, not only in the way in which modern Muslim writers regard the traditions of the past, but also in the practical sphere of law, and it is to these two matters that we will now turn.

At the present day it is to Pakistan that we must look for the clearest and most uncompromising attitude towards the traditions of the past and the influence of modern historical criticism. The first man to advocate a modern approach to education in India was Sir Sayyid Ahmad Khān (1817–98). His avowed object was to found a college where all that was best in Western thought could be taught in a Muslim atmosphere, and through his efforts what is now the University of Aligarh was founded. He held that it was impossible that there could be any contradiction between Islam and science, and he insisted that Islam was in conformity with nature. This, in effect, led him to deny the miraculous element in Islam, and he had to bear the full weight of the hostility of the ʿulamā. The influence of the school he founded was immense; one effect was to force earnest Muslims to consider seriously the social evils of polygamy, divorce, and slavery, and to adopt a critical attitude towards their traditional way of life and the authorities on which it was based.

He was followed by Sayyid Amīr ʿAlī, a Shīʿite, whose book, *The Spirit of Islam*, is one of the most widely read works in many Muslim countries. It demands that the Qurān shall be read without the interpretations put upon it by the ʿulamā, who represent the unauthorized teachings of their ancient predecessors. Thus he condemns polygamy on the authority of the Qurān, which, though it limited the number of wives to be kept at one time to four, ordered that if a man could not treat them all equitably and justly he must not marry more than one. He wrote: 'As absolute justice in matters of feeling is impossible the Koranic prescription amounted in reality to a prohibition.' (If polemic were the purpose of this book, one would be tempted to ask why, if a contingency is impossible, should the Qurān legislate for it.) He asserted that the blight which had fallen on the Muslim nations was due to the stranglehold of the past which prohibited the exercise of independent judgement, and ended with the expression of the hope that before long 'a general synod of Muslim doctors will authoritatively declare that polygamy, like slavery, is abhorrent to the laws of Islam.' In passing it may be noted that the right of independent judgement (*ijtihād*) is still to be vested in the *'ulamā*. His attitude towards the system of *purdah*, the seclusion of women, was that it was a temporary measure instituted by Muhammad. It was never intended to be a permanent institution, and it finds no place in the Qurān. This reformer went much further than any of his followers has been prepared to go: he regarded Muhammad as the author of the Qurān. I do not know of any modern writer who has taken the same view, though many Muslims hold the belief, and openly say so in conversation. There is no historical reason why they should not, because the doctrine that the Qurān is 'uncreate', i.e. literally the word of God, was not finally established until the third century of the *hijra*. Furthermore, I doubt whether very many Muslims would endorse his statement that 'except for the conception of the sonship of Jesus there is no fundamental difference between Christianity and Islam.' This much is true at least: the Qurān is nearer to Christianity than the system of Islam as it has developed through the centuries.

The next outstanding figure in Indian Islam is Sir Muhammad Iqbāl (1876–1938). He was a poet who wrote in Persian and Urdu and a philosopher who wrote in English. In 1928 he published *Six Lectures on the Reconstruction of Religious Thought in Islam*. Though Iqbāl has had considerable influence on the thought of the Indian Muslim, it may be doubted whether what he called a reconstruction will ever be regarded as such. When he comes down to details he is clear and explicit, but when dealing with general principles the poet and mystic come to the fore, and it is anything but easy to see what would be the practical outcome of his theories.

It must not be supposed that his work in any way resembles *The Revival of the Religious Sciences* by al-Ghazzālī, which was a systematic exposition of the faith and practice of a Muslim, his inner life, his aspirations, and his ultimate felicity. For the following summary of Iqbāl's lectures I have drawn freely on Professor Gibb's exposition of his system in his *Modern Trends in Islam*. Iqbāl asserted that the modern Muslim must study what Europe has thought, and work out how far European conclusions can help in the revision, and, if necessary, the reconstruction of theological thought in Islam. He must rethink the whole system of Islam without completely breaking with the past. But when Iqbāl applies himself to this task he leaves the forum of everyday life for the higher realms of Sūfī thought, tempered by the theories of some modern philosophers. He departs from orthodox Islam when he maintains that the Qurān teaches that the human ego possesses creative freedom. The Fall of Adam he interprets much as Christians do today, as a parable of 'man's rise from a primitive state of instinctive appetite to the conscious possession of a free self capable of doubt and disobedience', and 'the emergence of a finite ego which has the power to choose.' The Muslim doctrine of fatalism he regards as morally degrading, the invention of men with little grasp of philosophical truth. This is a doctrine which was, and is, fostered by vested interests. His teaching on heaven and hell has a familiar ring:

Heaven and hell are states, not localities. Their descriptions in the Qurān are visual representations of an inner fact, i.e., character. Hell, in the words of the Qurān, is 'God's kindled fire which mounts above the hearts' – the painful realization of one's failure as a man. Heaven is the joy of triumph over the forces of disintegration. There is no such thing as eternal damnation in Islam ...

Hell . . ., as conceived by the Qurān, is not a pit of everlasting torture inflicted by a revengeful God; it is a corrective experience which may make a hardened ego once more sensitive to the living breeze of Divine Grace. Nor is Heaven a holiday; Life is one and continuous . . ., Every act of a free ego creates a new situation, and thus offers further opportunities of creative unfolding.

It hardly needs saying that all this comes perilously near heresy in Islam. Iqbāl sees man as a 'co-worker' with God, a view which he bases on sūra 13 : 12, 'God will not change the condition of men until they change what is in themselves.' From this very brief summary of Iqbāl's theories the reader can see that he has left the Muslim with some principles based partly on texts which for generations have been interpreted in quite a different way, and partly on Christian thought in modern times.

One cannot but feel that when the practical application of his demand for a new interpretation of the Qurān in the light of modern needs comes into question Iqbāl hedges. He saw that the problem of adjustment was delicate and the responsibility of the reformer grave. Islam during the centuries had created 'something like a collective will and conscience'; therefore one has to recognize that 'even the immutability of socially harmless rules relating to food and drink, purity or impurity, has a life-value of its own.' It holds the complex society of Muhammadans together, and so one must be clear as to what its significance is before one tampers with it. But from there he goes on to say that the founders of the schools of law did not claim finality for their reasonings and interpretations. 'The claim of the present generation of Muslim Liberals to reinterpret the foundational legal principles in the light of their own experience and the altered conditions of modern life is, in my opinion, perfectly justified.' The Turkish poet and sociologist Ziya Gökalp had written a poem in which he asked how the *shariʿa* could regard women as contemptible. There must be equality in divorce, in separation, and in inheritance. Iqbāl says that he does not know whether equality in these matters is possible according to Muhammadan law. 'In view of the intense conservatism of the Muslims of India, Indian judges cannot but stick to what are called standard works.' This seems a poor stand to take after the brave words that have gone before; and it would be a poor consolation to a woman who had received half her brother's share of her father's property to be told that the rule 'does not assume the superiority of males over females, for such an assumption would be contrary to the spirit of Islam.' But here Iqbāl has overlooked the very definite statement of the Qurān that 'men have a status above women', [2:228]. In a short poem he says:

> I, too, am most sorrowful at the oppression of women;
> But the problem is intricate; no solution do I find possible.

This is the cry of one who cannot grapple with the tremendous force of inherited custom and practice.

And now let us turn to the immediate present. In 1948 Shaykh Muhammad Ashraf began the publication of a monthly journal called *The Islamic Literature*, with the declared objects of (1) reflecting in a worthy manner Islam's ambition to reconquer its lost field of cultural glory; (2) presenting the new interpretation of Islam that would fit in with the changed condition of the world; (3) analysing boldly and critically the present situation, unearthing the hidden treasures of Islam's *actual* past, ignorance of which has made Muslims feel so doubtful of their future; and (4) being a forum for scattered sections of the Muslim world to exchange views with one another in order to feel the reality of Islam's world-wide spiritual brotherhood. The journal is marked by a liberal and enlightened spirit, and though occasionally polemic raises its ugly head it is not the fault of the editor, whose style is always courteous. Articles from western Arabists are frequently to be found. I do not know of a parallel in a Christian periodical to this broad tolerance.

What is so attractive and refreshing is the editor's desire for truth; from the writings of other contributors we can see that there are many who share his convictions. After what has been said of the work of early reformers in the India of the British Empire it is easy to see its influence in the Pakistan of today. Much more will be said of Pakistan, not because it is part of the Commonwealth, but because it is unique among the Islamic nations in that it has come into being with the conscious and declared aim of showing the world what a free and enlightened Muslim State should be.

In a series of editorials Ashraf goes to the root of the matter – the authority of tradition. He takes a middle course: he will not follow the *ahl-e-Qurān* who reject the whole literature of tradition as a guide in the social life of the community, nor will he go with those slavish followers of tradition who would keep the Muhammadan world in the trammels of the past. He rejects the theory that revelation is of two kinds: that which is recited, i.e. the Qurān, and that which is not recited, i.e. the words of *hadīth*. The orthodox theory in effect is that both are of equal authority. 'Any society which desires to shape its legal and social structure on Islamic foundations must re-examine its attitude to *hadīth* and decide the matter with open eyes and unbiased mind.' 'What the prophet said or did, provided it has been correctly reported, is of great importance in explaining the real intent of the Qurān

and its detailed application in a particular historical situation.'
He makes the shrewd observation that had Qurān and *hadīth*
been of equal importance Muhammad's Companions would
have written down his sayings; but no Caliph or Companion
considered such a course necessary, whereas the Qurān was
written down in the time of Abū Bakr the first Caliph.
(Most Arabists would hold that only some chapters were
written down so early as this.) Had the early Muslims thought
that *hadīth* was as important as the Qurān they would have
taken steps to record it; but in fact they did not do so. It
cannot be argued that they refrained from doing so because
they themselves knew what the prophet had said, for if the
hadīth was as important as the Qurān the same measures
would have been taken to preserve it for posterity. 'They
could not have been so ignorant . . . as not to think that if an
event, talk, or deed is reported or recorded two hundred years
after its actual occurrence it is very likely that it may be mis-
reported or recorded inaccurately, not out of deliberate fal-
sification, but because man cannot hold in his brain the exact
picture of words uttered, or deeds done, one year ago, not to
speak of happenings in the dim past.' He argues that even the
most 'authentic' *hadīth* may have been the subject of misunderstanding and misrepresentation, and so *hadīth* can never
be anything but secondary to the Qurān. After exposing the
absurdity of particular *hadīth* the writer attacks the doctrine
that the Qurān can only be understood in the light of *hadīth*,
because the prophet was the best exponent of the Qurān. On
this argument, he says, the sayings of the Companions should
also be treated as on a par with the Qurān, because they would
have learned directly from the prophet himself; and similarly
their immediate followers, and we could go on and say that
every Imām and scholar who depends on these sources has

the same authority as the Qurān, 'because they constitute a necessary medium for understanding the Holy Book', and this is really what the *'ulamā* are driving at. Blind obedience to a chain of authorities of which they are the last link to be forged is their demand, and this is no better than ancestor-worship!

The writer goes on to point out that quite apart from the possible misunderstanding of the prophet's words and deeds as reported by the traditionists there is overwhelming evidence to prove that traditions were invented in the first Islamic centuries. Some of these, he rightly says, were the work of converts to Islam. They could not lay hands on the Qurān, so they got to work on tradition. (However, it should be added that some traditions from this source represent a high ethical standard, and others have been adopted and incorporated into the *sharī'a*.) He says, again rightly, that *hadīth* in praise of the Companions and the Ansār were inspired by group rivalry or by the politically ambitious or the party in power or the opposition. Many eschatological traditions are the reflexions of the general despair at the existing state of things when the Turks dominated the 'Abbāsid Caliphate. They put their expressions of horror and dismay into the mouth of the prophet. There is a tradition which says that if it were permissible for mankind to bow down to anyone but God 'I would have commanded women to bow down before their husbands.' This, says the writer, is in flagrant opposition to the Qurān, and undermines the whole structure of Islamic teaching in regard to the sexes (but see above). Again, 'If anything could be a bad omen it would be women and horses.' This is utterly foreign to the teaching of the prophet, and utterly beneath his dignity. 'Could he ever have thought of lumping together women and horses?' He finds it amazing that Muslims could believe that Qurān and *hadīth* were of equal rank when such stuff is found in collections of *hadīth* which are regarded as final and authentic. Once again the writer returns to the question whether *hadīth* is to be rejected altogether, as the *ahl-e-Qurān* desire, and he comes down decisively against such a course. With all its faults *hadīth* is part of Muslim history, indissolubly linked with the development of Muslims as a community. If it were rejected the *sharī'a* which is based on it would have to go too. What is wanted, he says, is a thorough examination of *hadīth* with a view to modifying and developing Muslim law so that it can be brought into living relation with modern thought and modern needs. To dispense with *hadīth* would be to deny that the personal example of the prophet had any value in the life of the Muslim. Therefore *hadīth* must be given a place next to the Qurān. 'Once it has been established that a particular *hadīth* or a set of them is really authentic, you have to accept it as the basis of law and practice.'

Here one must interpolate the question: How can one determine that a particular *hadīth* is authentic when practically all those which bear on law have *isnāds* which have satisfied those who scrutinized the credentials of the narrators? It is the view of most Arabists who have studied *hadīth* that though some must report what the prophet did and said, it is next to impossible to say which they are: in any case one would have to go behind the official collections to see what earlier writers have said, and they do not speak with one voice. (See Ch. 5.) One cannot but feel sympathy with the difficulty of would-be reformers. They know, as we know, that the edifice of *hadīth* was built up in the centuries following the prophet's death; but if they lay hands on any alleged authentic *hadīth*, then the whole edifice logically must collapse, and for a divinely ordered scheme of things provided by the 'ulamā they must substitute an arbitrary selection. This no doubt would be practical wisdom, but would it stand up to the criticism of the 'ulamā? If the course of the Western interpretation of Christianity is any guide – and there are many reasons why it need not be – there would be a movement like the Reformation in Europe which would leave the Muslim world divided into two sections: one holding fast to the traditions of the past and yielding nothing to modern thought; and another party like the ahl-e-Qurān, which the writer repudiates, going back to primitive Islam and making a fresh start from its holy book. In the middle would stand a body which clung to all that it thought true and of good report in the post-apostolic age, but repudiating the course of later tradition. It is this via media which Ashraf favours. He is not satisfied with the mere criticism of the chain of authorities for a particular tradition or group of traditions. He wants to apply the canons of historical and rational criticism to the contents of the hadīth. It is in the light of these principles that he presses for a fresh selection and codification of hadīth, so that the respect and confidence of educated Muslims would be won. To do this scholars with a progressive and enlightened outlook could formulate the principles of criticism, but they must not be men with 'a blind faith in the principles and values of Western capitalistic civilization.' In undertaking this task they should remember that the prophet applied the principles of Islam in a primitive stage of historical and social development which lacked the 'technical and organizational resources of the modern world.' This seems to mean that what was suitable and beneficial thirteen hundred years ago is no longer of value, and that it must be remembered that much of what tradition reports had a transitory value. He concludes: 'What we should do is to evolve fresh principle of historical and rational criticism, re-examine and re-codify the existing corpus of tradition, and then proceed on the basis of the holy Qurān and the *hadīth* so selected and codified towards a modification of the existing body of Islamic laws.' In this formidable task all men of good will would wish the Muslim community an abiding success. We shall see that already changes are being made in the *sharī'a* in various Islamic countries.

In Chapter 5 a sketch of the sources of Muslim law and of the formation of the four main schools has been given. In certain countries certain matters have been taken out of the purview of the *sharī'a* and now come within the scope of secular courts; but, broadly speaking, no change comparable with that which has taken and is taking place in Islamic countries today has been seen within Islam for a thousand years or more. Turkey, as everyone knows, has abolished the *sharī'a* altogether. Officially it is a secular State, though actually the influence of Islam on the population, especially in Asia, is very considerable, and shows signs of becoming stronger under the new democratic government.

In a series of articles in *The Muslim World* and elsewhere my colleague Mr J. N. D. Anderson has shown how in the Arab countries too the *sharī'a* is undergoing revision. Egypt, the Sudan, Syria, Lebanon, Jordan, and Iraq are all on the move. The changes which are being made illustrate how a definite attempt to relate the *sharī'a* to the conditions of modern life and to a more liberal view of human relations is being realized in positive legislation. It is abundantly clear that some hard thinking has preceded these changes, and one cannot but admire the ingenuity of the reformers. In brief, they have adopted the principle of searching for precedents not only in all the four schools but also in extinct schools like the Zāhirīs and some schismatic sects of the Shī'a. So, instead of each country following the laws of the school or schools predominant in that region, an eclectic system of legislation has been evolved. This method is not the innovation it would at first sight appear to be, because although some jurists hold that if a man was born in a certain school he must remain in it for the rest of his life, others allow him to change his school *in toto* but not in part. Others, and these provide the precedent behind modern eclecticism, maintained that a man could follow one school in one particular and another in others if his conscience so permitted. The practice of chopping and changing was called *talfīq*. However, this right applied to the individual: it did not apply to the *muftī* or *qāḍī*; he, as an officer responsible for the behaviour of the community and for giving it right guidance, was bound to follow the view of the school to which he belonged. Only the head of the State could override this obligation when the public interest so demanded. Controversy has raged round all these points. Modern legislators make no claim to the right of *ijtihād*. They claim that all that they have done is to choose between opinions and rival jurists, basing their choice on the principle that legislation must be brought into line with modern needs. Where their legislation clashes with *ijmā'*, as it sometimes does, they deny that there is any proof that a real consensus of opinion ever existed. If it did, why is there no express mention of it? It must be unanimous to be authoritative, and therefore it could only be binding if it could be proved to have existed on a given matter in the time of the Companions before they dispersed from Medina.

Some of the points which the reformers raise are of great importance and may well have far-reaching effects. For instance, they question how far commandments in the sacred texts are positive or permissive; do they mean You shall [not] or You may [not]? Are they matters of conscience which will be tried in heaven, or are they subject to the action of an earthly court? How far is a divine ordinance binding when the conditions under which it was promulgated have passed away?

In theory the *sharī'a* governs all man's activities; but in practice customary law survived, and the *sharī'a* was frequently set aside by the orders of the Caliphs and governors, especially where matters of commerce and criminal law were concerned. In the old Ottoman empire the commercial and penal codes formed on Western lines were established a century ago; and in Egypt in the 1870s a civil code based on the Code Napoléon was promulgated. From then to the present day there has been a progressive limitation of the scope of the *sharī'a* courts, which were left to deal with the vital personal matters of marriage, divorce, care of children, relatives, and inheritance. More recently jurisdiction in regard to gifts has been transferred from the *sharī'a* to the civil courts.

This eclectic method of revising the *sharī'a* is not new; it has a respectable history behind it. A century ago the Shaykh al-Islam at Constantinople ruled that a marriage of a woman who had been deserted by her husband could be dissolved by the courts. This was in face of the contrary ruling of the Hanafī school, which was the official school of the Ottoman empire, but in agreement with the other three schools. In order not to put pressure on Hanafī judges it was held that the *qādī* of another school must judge the case and give his decision. In 1915 a wife was permitted dissolution of marriage if her husband suffered from certain specific diseases.

One great change which has taken place in the Near East

is the institution of Courts of Appeal. The *shariʿa* knows of no such courts, and therefore it is an innovation; and innovations are generally branded as heretical. This novelty, however, has excited little opposition, because it is obvious to the majority of Muslims that it is a change in the public interest.

In Egypt a most ingenious way of by-passing the *shariʿa* has been worked out. The law has been left unaltered, but the judges have been forbidden to entertain certain actions. Child marriage is repugnant to modern Egyptians, but they could hardly prohibit the practice in view of the fact that Muhammad married ʿĀʾisha when she was but a child playing with her dolls. Instead, in 1923, they decreed that the courts must not give a hearing to any action (other than a claim of paternity) where the wife was under 16 and the husband under 18 years of age at the time of the marriage; nor were officials allowed to register marriages of young people under these ages. The Code of Procedure, 1931, went further and refused to allow the courts to try such cases unless the parties had reached these ages at the time of the action; nor could they give a hearing to actions from parties whose marriages had not been registered. Obviously this method of suppressing undesirable and pernicious and harmful laws is capable of extension. By denying justice to anyone who has acted contrary to what is felt to be the public weal those who encourage child marriages are likely to think twice before they go further; if they wish to marry or give in marriage they may do so because the law allows it, but they do so at their own risk.

The most important legislation of recent times was the Ottoman Law of Family Rights promulgated in 1917. This law of course no longer obtains in the country of its origin, but it is still applied in Lebanon and has only recently been superseded by even more progressive codes in Syria and Jordan. It forbids the marriage of boys and girls who have not reached the age of puberty. An explanatory memorandum is added to this law. It bases its action in regard to child marriage on humanistic grounds when it says that it is pathetic that a child who should be playing happily in the streets should be made to perform the heaviest of all duties, the bearing of children and the management of a home. As a result of this deplorable state of affairs the mother becomes a nervous wreck and the children are weak and feeble. The writers attribute the deterioration of Muslim stock to this practice. It is prescribed that marriages shall be contracted after public notice has been given, and a proper registration of the marriage is incumbent on the duly appointed authority. Nevertheless there is only one marriage which is null and void (whether the parties are under age or within the prohibited relationship or whether the woman is a fifth wife or married under compulsion), and that is the marriage of a Muslim woman to a non-Muslim. All other marriages, however incestuous or violent, are irregular: they are not invalid. It is also provided that if a woman stipulates in her marriage contract that her husband shall not take a second wife during her lifetime the contract is valid and the stipulation is recognized. Several attempts to make this the law in Egypt have been attempted, but have hitherto failed; on one occasion only the royal prerogative prevented the Act from becoming the law of the land. A husband is bound to dower his wife and maintain her, and reciprocal rights of inheritance are established between them on marriage. She is bound to cohabit with her husband unless she cannot do so for no fault of her own, such as sickness, imprisonment, and so on. Neither can compel the other to accommodate his or her relatives in their home without the consent of the other. If a husband refuses to maintain his wife she can get an order from the court. (Further information on the kind of actions which arise from such laws, the amount of maintenance, how to recover it if the husband has decamped, and so on, will be found in Mr Anderson's articles referred to above.)

In the case of divorced mothers the Egyptian Law of 1929 allowed the court at its discretion to award the custody of children to their mother up to the age of 9 (instead of 7) in the case of a boy, and 11 (instead of 9) in the case of a girl. In the Sudan it was decreed that girls might be left with their mothers until they marry, and boys until they attain puberty. Most of these reforms have been introduced by adopting the most humane decision in any one of the four schools.

Recent years have brought some amelioration of the hard lot of women in Muslim countries in the matter of divorce. Under the Hanafi law – and this, be it remembered, obtains in the greater part of the Muslim world – a husband may divorce his wife for any reason or for no reason at all. The effect of this is to preclude remarriage, if the man regrets his action, until she has consummated a marriage with another man and then been divorced by him. The husband can divorce his wife by simply saying so three times. On the other hand, a woman can never divorce her husband on any ground whatever, unless she has his permission to do so. Nor can she get a judicial dissolution of marriage for neglect, ill-treatment, or positive cruelty. All she can do is to apply to the courts for maintenance if she has been deserted, and for the trial of her husband if he has treated her with undue violence and there are witnesses to that effect. If her husband suffers from an infectious and loathsome disease she cannot get a divorce. The sole ground for divorce (apart from child marriages before the age of puberty) is sexual impotence on the man's part. What seems to the Western reader incomprehensible in this system is the fact that this state of affairs can co-exist with the recognition of the *hadīth* 'Of the things which are lawful the most hateful to God is divorce', which is often quoted with approval.

In our eyes an extraordinary feature of the Hanafī system is that a divorce uttered in jest and not meant seriously is just as binding as a deliberate utterance. But this is not all. Even a divorce spoken when a man is drunk is valid if he was culpably drunk, and so, too, is a divorce uttered under compulsion. The logic behind all this is that divorce is a serious matter, and a man cannot escape the consequences of his action. What is lost sight of is the fact that it is the woman who suffers for it. The only deterrent against divorce is the power of the woman's guardian to insist at the time of marriage on a larger dower, part of which is to be paid down, while the remainder must be paid if she is divorced or if her husband dies. This stipulation has discouraged divorce among the moneyed classes, but obviously it would have little or no effect among the fellahin, who live from hand to mouth.

Enlightened Muslim opinion today, however, is not satisfied with this state of things. Some salutary adjustments were made in India in 1939, and ten years earlier the Egyptian Legislature passed an Act which declared that a divorce pronounced by a drunken man is invalid, and so is a divorce uttered under compulsion. The latter is the view of the other three schools, while the former is supported by the minority view, which is that a man who does not know what he is doing is not to be held responsible for his words; but he can and should be punished for drinking prohibited liquors. A new view is taken of 'conditional' divorce. If a man says to his wife, 'If you do such and such a thing you are divorced' and she does it, no divorce ensues, except in the unlikely event that the husband wishes to end the marriage in any case.

It has hitherto been recognized that the triple formula of divorce pronounced on one occasion is effective, but the new law goes back to earlier days when it was held that a triple divorce on one occasion was merely the equivalent of a single pronouncement and was therefore revocable. These reforms have gone some way towards relieving wives of the intolerable strain caused by the fear of divorce which hangs over their heads day and night; for the position of a divorced woman in a Muslim country who is not likely to find another husband in middle or old age is utterly miserable. She is left in penury, and must return in disgrace to her father's house if he is still alive. If he or her nearest male relation is a poor man he cannot keep her, and so she is bound to endure every form of humiliation and actual suffering. The new law, by insisting that where the triple divorce has been pronounced on a single occasion it can only count as a single pronouncement, brings into operation a waiting period called 'idda, which lasts for three months or, if the woman is pregnant, until her confinement. During this period her husband must maintain her, and she may not remarry; and he may revoke his divorce. The practice of marriage with another man after divorce to make it possible for the woman to remarry her first husband is intensely disliked by most modern Muslims. Divorce now must be pronounced at the correct time, and the 'idda must be properly observed. If the divorce is pronounced once a month until the final and irrevocable third formula has been spoken it is fairly certain that there is little hope of the parties living happily together. On the whole, the law of Egypt is more humane than that obtaining in most Muslim countries.

Egyptians are fully alive to the social evils of divorce, and draft legislation put forward in 1943 and 1945 goes much more thoroughly into the whole question. The first proposal was that no divorce should be registered without the consent of the local *qāḍī*. A man could disregard this order and his divorce would be valid, but he would be liable to a fine or imprisonment or both. Here again we see how the main structure of the *sharī'a* is left intact, but the application of it when it is harmful to society is made all but impossible. The second proposal was that before the *qāḍī* gave his consent to the divorce he should examine the cause of dissension between the parties and try his utmost to reconcile them. Up to the present these proposals have not received the assent of the legislature.

Women now get a divorce from their husband: (*a*) if he fails to maintain them; (*b*) if he suffers from a serious physical defect; (*c*) for ill-treatment; and (*d*) for desertion. (The three schools allowed divorce where the husband was unable to provide his wife with the necessities of life.) The Egyptian Act of 1920 disregards the arguments and exceptions of the schools, and gives the wife a divorce if the husband fails to maintain her, though if he can prove that he is destitute he is given a month's grace. A husband undergoing a prison sentence and thus unable to support his wife may find himself divorced when he returns to everyday life. The scale of maintenance is fixed according to the husband's means. So far as physical defects are concerned we have seen that the Hanafī school recognized only sexual impotence as a valid cause for divorce. The other three schools admitted a number of loathsome diseases on the ground that the prophet sent away one of his wives who was suspected of having leprosy. They argued that such diseases as cause physical repulsion and endanger the health of offspring were valid impediments, but if a woman knew beforehand that her husband suffered from one of these diseases she had no redress. The new law allows dissolution of marriage in such cases. Ill-treatment now gives ground for divorce. But it must be remembered that the Qurān allows a husband to chastise his wife for disobedience. A great many differences of opinion about the kind of punishment admissible and the offences for which such punishment may be meted out have been expressed. Anything that comes within the bounds of lawful punishment is not ill-treatment in the meaning of the law. The situation now is that the *qādī* may grant a woman a divorce if she can prove ill-treatment and if he cannot reconcile the parties. If he refuses her petition and she applies for divorce once more he must appoint two arbitrators. If they cannot bring the two together they shall recommend a divorce and the court will act on this. Where the husband has deserted his wife but has left money for her maintenance the new law allows divorce after a year or more.

The effect of these enactments is to give a considerable measure of relief to wives, and, apart from the ultra-conservative party, they have been generally welcomed. Many Muslims do not think that the reforms have gone far enough. Others have criticized the amendments on the ground that they violate the true conception of marriage, which entails mutual love and devotion. They agree that cruelty or the concealment of a loathsome disease at the time of marriage or culpable negligence in providing for a wife's maintenance are such crimes as make married life in the true sense of the word impossible; but they hold that it is wrong to grant a woman a divorce if her unfortunate husband suddenly loses his money through no fault of his own, and they deprecate releasing a wife from her obligations if her husband has contracted a serious disease after marriage again through no fault of his. Morally these arguments are unanswerable, and the only criticism that could be levelled against them is that the man is still perfectly free to get rid of his wife at any time if he keeps within the rules laid down in the Act.

In the matter of testamentary bequests Egypt has advanced far beyond many Muslim countries. It now allows a man to leave up to one-third of his property to an heir as well as a non-heir whether the other heirs consent or not. (Of course it would be asking too much of human nature in any country east or west to expect heirs to agree to the alienation of part of their inheritance if they had the power to veto it, as they had in Egypt until the passing of the Act in 1945.) This provision is in opposition to what has hitherto been regarded as the consensus of the community based on certain traditions attributed to the prophet. The legislators give their reasons, and they are good reasons. They say that if a man distributes his property item by item among his heirs as he thinks best, litigation and quarrelling are avoided. Moreover, the testator now has the right to take into consideration the property and wealth of his heirs and to allot his estate in the way best suited to their needs and wants. If such bequests were subject to the consent of *all* the other heirs, those who stand in the greatest need would be deprived of help. They boldly assert that they have made this law in the public interest. No legal precedent is quoted in support of this innovation, but reference is made to the Qurān, 2:176, which lays down that a man must bequeath his property equitably to his parents and kindred. The orthodox view is that this verse was abrogated by the 'Verses of Inheritance', 4:8 ff.; but the reformers deny that there is any evidence for this assertion. It is interesting to note that Ibn Qutayba (d. A.H. 276) could get rid of the doctrine that testamentary disposition was commanded in the Qurān only by asserting that that verse was abrogated and the tradition, 'There can be no testamentary disposition in favour of an heir', showed that the *sunna* abrogated the Qurān. This was the very point which his opponents contested.

No provision is made in the qurānic law of inheritances for a man's grandchildren by a deceased son if no other son survives or by a deceased daughter if there is no agnate or quota-heir whatever. The new law provides that if the deceased has made no provision for such grandchild or grandchildren the court must allot to them the share that would have belonged to their parent had he been living, but it must not exceed one-third. If they had received from the deceased during his lifetime some gift, this must be taken into account in giving them what they are entitled to. Up to the present it has not been possible to deal with the hardship of the grandchildren of deceased parents mentioned above, for the simple reason that the Qurān makes no provision for them. The Egyptian law has met the difficulty by bringing it under the heading of bequests, which it has made lawful, and this it was able to do by declining to agree that the verse of bequests was repealed by the verses of inheritance.

Mortmain has always constituted a grave problem. Europe has suffered grievously from it. In Islam, as mortmain is an integral part of the *sharī'a*, it could not be tackled without serious opposition from vested interests. Briefly, the system, called *waqf*, is that a man may leave his property as a pious benefaction in perpetuity to a religious institution or for a religious purpose such as a mosque, school, hospital, or even public works; or he may leave it in perpetuity for the use of members of his family. The bequest is irrevocable. The *waqf* is administered by an official who is paid for his services. In the course of the centuries these benefactions became so enormous that a separate ministry was needed to cope with them, and abuses of every kind and description grew up. An immense amount of landed property came under this administration, and often deteriorated in value and productivity through bad and corrupt management, so that the original purpose of the donors was frustrated and the country suffered from the poor use of its land. It has been estimated that no less than three-quarters of the whole of the arable land of the old Ottoman empire was controlled by *waqf*.

European powers were the first to deal with the problem. In Algeria the institution was brought under French law, so that the land could be farmed to the best advantage; and in Morocco the *waqf* land became the property of the occupier under certain conditions. Turkey abolished the Ministry of Waqfs in 1924, and later ordered that the estates must be sold and worked for the public advantage. The reform of the system in Egypt was begun by the great Muhammad 'Alī, who confiscated all agricultural land under *waqf* and compensated the beneficiaries. Since 1924 the Ministry of Waqfs has been under the control of parliament to the great advantage of the country.

The evils of the system despite its pious origin have been apparent to Muslims for centuries. Administrators proved dishonest and incompetent could not be dealt with by any authority. Moreover, the country suffered in that the land was not properly cultivated, houses were allowed to fall into ruin, and, in short, none of the steps necessary to utilize to the full the resources of the country were taken for lack of initiative and incentive. In 1949 Syria prohibited the creation of family *waqfs* altogether and provided for the liquidation of those already existing. In Egypt there was a strong feeling in favour of the abolition of the system lock, stock, and barrel, but the opposition of the ʿ*ulamā* was strong enough to persuade the reformers that they had better take a middle course. Accordingly in 1946 an interim measure was passed which dealt with the worst of the abuses. Its authors honestly tried to retain all that was good in the old system and to change the law in such a way as to serve the original purpose of the donors and the best interest of the community. Under this law any new *waqf* could only be valid after a declaration in a *sharīʿa* court. It leaves a *waqf* in favour of a mosque untouched, but a family *waqf* is no longer perpetual: it can pass only to two series of beneficiaries. This is one of the greatest changes the new law brings about. It would serve no good purpose to review this Act in detail. Suffice it to say that throughout the larger interests of the country are kept steadily in view. Details like the repairs of buildings, reinvestment of monies, restrictions placed on beneficiaries, and so on – all matters which the legal tradition a thousand years ago could hardly be expected to deal with – are governed in the light of this principle. Recent legislation in Egypt has abolished private *waqfs* altogether. Syria has done the same.

The law in the Lebanon since 1949 has followed the same general line, and in the Sudan recent legislation has adopted the same pattern though not always in the direction of greater freedom for women. Jordan in 1951 brought in new legislation on family rights. Clearly this is based on the Ottoman Law of Family Rights, and has kept a close eye on the developments in Egypt. For example, the normal minimum age for marriage is 18 and 17 for a boy and girl respectively, though subject to the permission of the court a girl may be married at 15. Other changes indicate the awakening of a social conscience. Divorce to be effective must be pronounced on three separate occasions; a *qādī* may not sanction the marriage of a girl to a man more than 20 years her senior unless it is proved to his satisfaction that she is completely willing and has not been forced to agree under pressure. A greater innovation is that if a woman stipulates in her marriage contract that she shall have the right to divorce her husband; or that he shall not compel her to leave the town where it was agreed that they should live; or that he shall not take to himself a second wife, if the stipulation has been registered in the certificate of marriage, it must be respected and the marriage shall be dissolved at the request of the wife. A considerable improvement in the lot of women is brought about by the Jordanian law in regard to separation for cruelty, maintenance, the payment of a midwife, and so on. In the matter of divorce the new legislation follows fairly closely the Egyptian system; when it departs therefrom it is in the direction of helping the woman, who is always at a disadvantage in the matter of divorce.

Events move more slowly in Iraq, where governments change fairly rapidly and the Sunnīs and Shīʿīs are often at variance. Nevertheless a draft Code of Personal Law was approved by a judicial committee of the Iraq parliament in 1947. It still awaits ratification. It must be remembered that Iraq has not enjoyed a system of higher education such as has been in vogue in Egypt for some generations, and so the weight of opposition from the 'old guard' is inevitably greater. The codification of the law would deprive many of their livelihood, for there would be no need to seek the ruling of the 'ulamā, who alone know the intricacies of the ancient law books, while it would seem to be an invasion of the prerogative of the Ja'farīs who still claim the right of *ijtihād*. However, the report having been shelved for a time by parliament and sent back to the committee to consider amendments may possibly become the law of the land in the not too distant future.

This code differs from those we have been considering because it has to deal with both Sunnīs and Shī'īs, and where no compromise is possible the code enacts that they shall be dealt with according to their own tradition. Generally speaking, it may be said that the code for Sunnīs follows the laws in the Ottoman Law of Family Rights and the recent Egyptian reforms. Marriages must be registered and stipulations in the marriage contract must be kept. Whether this applies to the conditions made by the bride as to monogamy, cruelty, and so on is not clear. On the other hand, a guardian is allowed to marry a child, though the husband is forbidden access to her until she has reached the age of puberty. Obviously this provision could easily be abused, and here the code lacks the humane element in the Egyptian and Turkish laws. When non-Muslims marry and one of them accepts Islam, if the other refuses to follow suit the union is automatically dissolved. Where the two parties cannot live together peaceably family arbitrators are to endeavour to reconcile them. If they fail the *qādī* may decree a divorce. The laws on the pronouncement of divorce by the husband follow the Egyptian model, though the Shī'īs still retain the laws peculiar to them. A woman may claim a divorce if her husband is impotent or suffers from a noxious disease; similarly if her husband fails to support her.

In regard to inheritance it is laid down that a man may

leave up to one-third of his property by will to whom he wishes. This, like the Egyptian law to the same effect, involves a break with the *shari'a* as it has hitherto been interpreted. But there is this difference, that in Ja'farī law it has always been the practice, and in a country composed of large numbers of the two great divisions of Islam it would be easier to make the law of one half of the population apply to the whole. Obviously where a Sunnī is fettered and a Shī'ī is free to do what he likes with his money within certain limits, some of the population must often have reflected on the injustice of a law which did not bind millions of their fellow-citizens while holding them in its grip.

From all this it can be seen that the criticism of the old system built up in the early centuries of Islam is slowly yielding to the efforts of reformers. After all, the evolution of law is a slow process, and one cannot expect a rapid advance when all the powers of church and tradition can be marshalled against any proposal that is not in keeping with the corpus of tradition on which theoretically the law is based. However, it will have become evident that much has been done and that more will be done to bring the law of the Muhammadan peoples into line not only with modern needs but also with modern consciences. Two major reforms have been recommended by responsible authority in Egypt. It has been noted that the Egyptian cabinet in 1926 approved draft legislation which made it obligatory for a man wishing to take a second wife to get the *qādī*'s permission, and forbade the latter to give such consent unless he was satisfied that the applicant could support all his dependants adequately and also appeared likely to be able to treat two wives equitably. Further, it recommended that no husband should be able to divorce his wife without the consent of the court, which would investigate the circumstances and try to bring the two parties together before allowing a divorce. Any infringement of this rule was to be punished by fine or imprisonment. These two salutary laws have not yet been ratified.

It would be rash to expect too much from the Muslim world as a whole in these matters. The forces of reaction are enormously strong, and are firmly entrenched in every country except Turkey. In Sa'ūdī Arabia they are all-powerful. Still, the advance of knowledge, the influence of the press, and the success of the reforms which have already been brought about should do much to dispose even the most conservative Muslims to re-examine the foundations on which their edifice has been built.

It has been pointed out that one of the Egyptian reforms in legislation in the matter of testamentary bequests was carried through despite the fact that it runs contrary to the doctrine of the 'ulamā that one verse in the Qurān was abrogated by others. Strange as it may seem, the doctrine has been held for more than a thousand years that a large number of verses have been abrogated. So strongly is the principle entrenched that some medieval writers have gone so far as to say that it is unlawful for any person who does not know what verses abrogate others to comment on the Qurān. Modern Egyptians are not the only Muslims to react against this doctrine. In the Pakistani journal *The Islamic Literature*, to which we have already referred, more than once one writer has set out the evidence in favour of a doctrine and another has written a reply in which he endeavours to show that no such cancellation exists or ever has existed. If we look at the question dispassionately we see that the evidence is both internal and external, though not all the arguments that have been adduced in favour of abrogation appear to be cogent.

There are two passages in the Qurān which would seem to favour the belief that abrogation is to be found there. The first (2:105) runs: 'If we abrogate or cause any verse to be forgotten we will replace it by a better one or one similar.' In its context, as the opponent of the thesis says, it is possible that abrogation here refers to the Jewish and Christian scriptures, and the fair-minded will give a verdict of not proven. But 16:103, 'If we substitute one verse for another', can hardly refer to any other book than the Qurān. This evidently was the opinion of the *'ulamā*, who proceeded to act on it in their exegesis and their system of law; e.g.

(1) The celebrated 'Verse of the Sword' (9:5), 'Slay the polytheists wherever you find them', is said to have cancelled no less than one hundred and twenty-four verses which enjoined toleration and patience. The opponent of abrogation denies that there is any contradiction here, on the ground that the overriding commandment is to forgive enemies and to endure hardships for God's sake. He writes: 'This is rather a sign of strength than weakness.' The sword is to come into play only when there is an enemy who seeks to destroy Islam. This seems to me not only a legitimate interpretation of the apparent inconsistency, but also one worthy of general acceptance. The *'ulamā* by encouraging a violent and fanatical spirit have given Muhammadanism a sinister reputation contrary to many precepts of its founder. Of course to the Western reader there is no difficulty whatever in reconciling a broad tolerance towards others with war against the enemies of human freedom. But it is much more difficult to adjust the words of a book which has been dictated by God himself. An inspired man can err at times: an inspired book cannot. Therefore on this theory one must, I think, hold with the *'ulamā* that the sword is decreed; but if we adopt a modern

view that in the changing circumstances toleration of paganism and hostility to monotheism that threatened the existence of the Islamic community had to cease and give way to armed conflict, there is no contradiction whatever in the Qurān on this matter.

(2) ' [Fast] a certain number of days, but if any one of you is ill or on a journey then [he must fast] the same number of days [later on] ; and for those who can afford it there is a ransom, the feeding of one poor person ... But to fast is better for you did you but know it' (2:180). This verse is said to be cancelled by 2:195, 'Whosoever of you is present in the month, let him fast; and he who is ill or on a journey shall fast a similar number of days [later on].' Here one can hardly escape the conclusion that the first verse allows a rich man to buy himelf out of the fast, while the second is a general order excluding only the sick and travellers, and then only for the period during which fasting would be dangerous or impossible. This was the view of one learned commentator, who explained the situation thus: 'He who likes, fasts; and he who likes, feeds a poor person.' However you look at these verses they cannot be squared: in one the rich can evade the fast; in the other they cannot; and it is going beyond the evidence to say with the apologist that the exception applies to the sick and to travellers. Quite clearly it does not. Therefore one must agree in this instance that the 'ulamā are right in holding that one verse cancels the other.

(3) The relation of bequests to the law of inheritance has already been discussed.

(4) It has been held that the law allowing the prophet an unlimited number of wives (33:50) was revoked by 33:52, which prohibited him from having any more from that time onwards. The apologist seems to have common sense on his

side when he says that there is no revocation, and that the verse that comes later on in the chapter is later in its application. Muhammad was allowed to keep the number of wives he had, though it was in excess of the number permitted to anyone else, but he was not allowed henceforth to add to his harem. A great many other verses are alleged to be cancelled; but from what has been said it is clear that on the orthodox theory of the inspiration of the Qurān it does abrogate itself: from the point of view of common sense and the application of general principles to everyday life it is perfectly straightforward.

When we come to look at the external evidence there is considerable justification for the belief that the Qurān was subject to alteration in its initial stages; indeed the large number of variants, not always trifling in significance, confirms the assumption. First of all, there is the notorious verse (53:19 f.) 'Have you considered al-Lāt and al-'Uzzā and Manāt the third other?' which was once followed by the words 'Verily they are the exalted maidens and their intercession is to be hoped for.' The earliest authority on the life of Muhammad asserts that these words were uttered by Muhammad at the instigation of Satan, and caused enormous satisfaction among the heathen Meccans and corresponding dismay among his own followers. What gave special significance to these words was the fact that they were those of the chant of the Quraysh as they processed round the Ka'ba. The Qurān has made a slight alteration and a significant omission: instead of saying 'By al-Lāt', etc., it reads, 'Have you considered al-Lāt', etc., and the sentence about the exalted maidens is dropped altogether. Subsequently Gabriel came to the prophet and denied that he had revealed the words to him. The apologist is at a disadvantage here. All he can do is to say that the whole story is the invention of polytheists and hypocrites. But abuse of the plaintiff seldom helps the defence. Ibn Ishāq, the reporter of the story, is the man on whom everyone relies for the details of the prophet's life; and Wāqidī is a trustworthy reporter of traditions from early sources, though his reputation is low among those who dislike his frankness and disregard for the notions of those who were born a century or so after his death; while Tabarī, the third offender in recording the incident, is a most impartial historian who recorded what he had heard and read. You cannot get behind these sources. There are no good grounds for asserting that these men were not good Muslims, and as such it is impossible to suggest a motive that would induce them to write such a story about the prophet unless it were true. They were probably proud that Muhammad should have been thought so formidable an adversary that Satan had to come in person to oppose his message. Why, then, should they conceal an event which so redounded to his credit, for Satan's effort ended in failure? All this happened long before the doctrine of the eternity of the Qurān became a rigid dogma. For these reasons if historical evidence is to be given any value we must hold that Muhammad pronounced these words in the middle of sūra 53. Whether they were ever existent in a written copy is impossible to say.

With these words the prophet's biographer connected sūra 22:51, 'Whenever we sent a messenger or a prophet before you when he urgently desired something [in this case the conversion of the Meccans by a compromise] Satan interjected something into his desire; but God abrogates what Satan interjects; then God establishes his verses.' Nevertheless, says the author in 4:41, 'It is a mighty book; falsehood cannot come at it from front or rear. It is a revelation from the Wise, the Praised One.'

Again, there is a tradition from 'Ā'isha, the prophet's wife, that a certain chapter which now consists of 73 verses once contained no less than 200, and that when 'Uthmān compiled the Qurān the missing verses could not be found. One of them was called the Verse of Stoning, and is said to have contained the order to stone a man or woman who had committed adultery. It cannot be affirmed with any certainty that this verse ever formed part of the Qurān; it is more likely that it was either a genuine *hadīth* of the prophet or a very early invention of one of his followers. The fact remains that this verse is said to have been part of the original Qurān. Many early authorities say so, and what is very significant is that the first Caliphs punished adulterers by stoning; this is still the penalty prescribed in Muslim law-books, whereas the Qurān (24:2) prescribes a hundred stripes. In this case there is not sufficient evidence in favour of abrogation to claim it as a proof, though it remains to be explained why, if the Qurānic penalty is scourging the *sharī'a* should decree stoning.

The canonical traditionists report that 4:95 was dictated by the prophet to his amanuensis Zayd thus: 'Those believers who sit at home are not equal to those who fight in the way of God with their goods and their persons.' A blind man was present and heard the words. He immediately interjected that were he as other men he would certainly fight; whereupon the prophet interposed the words 'except those who suffer from a grave impediment' which stand in the text today. The apologist can only call this a false calumny; but again it seems impossible to suggest a reason why the story should have been invented.

The reader must now form his own opinion on these matters of such great moment to Muslims. The editor of *The Islamic Literature* says that if the first article were accepted without reservation it would destroy the very basis of Islam, and he regards *hadīth* as responsible for the doctrine of abrogation and most of the sectarian ideas. This seems to be putting the cart before the horse; the traditions were invented to justify the doctrines and laws of the sects; but, after all, the practical outcome would be the same if the stranglehold of *hadīth* on the Muslim community were loosened, and that, as the editor sees, is the task before Muhammadans today.

Muslims are intensely conscious of their decline from the great days of the Islamic empire, and a host of writers have analysed the causes which have led to their decline. The tendency now is to repudiate the teaching of the past on fatalism, the inferiority of women, blind obedience to authority, lack of a healthy spirit of scepticism, and a low public morality. Contact with the West has stimulated self-criticism, and there are not wanting signs that the new generation is determined to put an end to this state of affairs if it possibly can. Women must be freed from imprisonment which has condemned them to a life of ignorance and frustration, and they must be allowed to go out into the world and take their proper place in society. A spirit of co-operation with non-Muslims is advocated. The exploitation of the poor peasant by the rich landlord must no longer be tolerated, otherwise Islam will be crushed between the Communists on the one hand and the *ʿulamā* on the other, for the *ʿulamā* are at the back of the rich. Some of these writers are outspoken to a degree, and their condemnation of the existing state of society is even more thoroughgoing than those of Christian missionaries a generation or two ago. The difference is that they indignantly reject the suggestion that the religion of Islam is responsible for these evils, and they put the blame on the Muslims who fail to live up to the principles of their religion.

It is clear from what these modern writers say that the ill-informed fear of some European writers that the Islamic peoples may become Communists is utterly unfounded. The Bolshevik régime in Turkistan is bitterly resented. There the rulers are said to have made a systematic attack on Islam, shooting the local leaders, razing the mosques, and burning the Qurān, employing in these tasks young men whom they have indoctrinated with atheism. The religious leader appointed by the Soviet Government (his name is given) is said to be a secret agent of the police. The writer's attitude to this is summed up in his words: 'The liberation of Turkistan from Russian rule will without doubt lead to an Islamic revival.'

It would be a rash man who would prophesy concerning the outcome of the struggle between the reformers, the selfish rich, and the 'ulamā; but provided that the former have a sufficiently large audience to whom they can appeal through the radio and the press, there would seem to be good ground for hope that the next few years will see a gradual reinterpretation of Islam and far-reaching reforms in the structure of society. The history of Islam has shown that it has extraordinary powers of adaptation: it has succeeded in absorbing apparently incompatible philosophies, and mutually contradictory religious conceptions, and it has silently abandoned others which it has tried and found wanting. Its one danger is that the old forces of reaction will be too strong for the new spirit of liberalism, armed as they are with shibboleths and anathemas which can rouse the ignorant masses and terrorize men of vision. Only time can show which party will gain the upper hand.

THE RELATION OF ISLAM TO CHRISTIANITY

THE brief statement which follows is not a polemic in any sense of the word, but a purely objective summary of the relation between the two religions. It is impossible to write of Islam without saying something about its predecessors, if only because the Qurān claims to confirm and to correct the earlier scriptures of Jews and Christians.

Perhaps the most direct way of indicating the relation would be to take the Apostles' Creed, as the document regarded by practically all Christians as an authoritative summary of their faith, and see how far the Qurān agrees with it (the words in italics are rejected by Islam):

I believe in God
the Father
Almighty, Maker of heaven and earth:
And in Jesus Christ
His only Son, our Lord,
Who was conceived by the Holy Ghost, Born of the Virgin Mary,
Suffered under Pontius Pilate, Was crucified
Dead? *and buried, He descended into hell; The third day*
He rose again from the dead,
He ascended into heaven,
And sitteth on the right hand of God the Father Almighty;
From thence He shall come
to judge the quick and the dead.
I believe in the Holy Ghost;
The Holy Catholic Church;
The Communion of Saints;
The Forgiveness of sins;
The Resurrection of the body, And the life everlasting.

If we went outside the Qurān for parallels with Christian doctrine we should find some, but we should enter into the field of controversy, and therefore these notes will be confined exclusively to what the Qurān itself says on the subjects which fall within the scope of the Apostles' Creed.

The Father. This is a term abhorrent to Muslims in reference to God, because it is understood in the sense of physical generation, and to say that God is a father implies to them that he must have a wife: therefore on that ground they are perfectly right in rejecting the term as blasphemous. Nor do they admit the term in the metaphorical sense that God is the father of all men, who stand to him in the relation of children.

Jesus Christ is believed to be an apostle sent by God. He is a man and the slave of God.

Conceived by the Holy Ghost. Cf. sūra 21, 'We breathed into her who was chaste of Our Spirit, and we made her and her son a sign (*āya*) to the worlds.' This inbreathing of the divine spirit is recorded also of the creation of Adam (15:29): 'And when I have made him a complete man and breathed into him of My Spirit, fall you down prostrating yourselves to him.' It is clear from these two passages that the Holy Spirit is not necessarily a person, but rather an emanation. In Islam in other texts it is understood to be Gabriel, because it is he that communicated the Qurān to Muhammad in 2:291, while in 16:104 it is the Holy Spirit. Similarly 19:17 reads, 'We sent to her Our spirit and he took the form of a full-grown man.' Further 4:169 says of Jesus: 'The Messiah, the Son of Mary, is only the apostle of God and His Word which He cast to Mary and a spirit from Him. So believe in God and His apostles and do not say "Three". Forbear! (it is) better for you. Allāh is only One God; so transcendent is He that He cannot have a Son.' The conception of spirit in the Qurān is difficult to follow. Other passages speak of angels being sent down with the spirit to whom God wills of his creatures.

The 'Holy Spirit' is mentioned four times in the Qurān: 2:81, 'We gave Jesus the Son of Mary the plain indications and strengthened him with the Holy Spirit', and similarly 5:109. But all true believers are strengthened with the Holy Spirit, cf. 58:22 and 16:104.

The most that can be said is that it is the plain teaching of the Qurān that, as St Paul said, Jesus is the Second Adam in that he was created by the immediate action of God through his breath, and not by human generation. It cannot be said that it teaches that the Holy Spirit is God himself: he is the breath or wind of God.

Virgin Mary. The virginity of Mary is taught almost in the words of Luke 1:34 in sūra 19:20; and 66:12 says that 'she was chosen and purified by God.'

Was crucified. 4:155 ff. explicitly deny the crucifixion in the words 'They did not kill him and they did not crucify him, but one was made to resemble him' (or, perhaps, 'they thought they did').

Dead. In spite of the denial of the crucifixion, there are some passages which speak of the death of Jesus, who is said to have said, 'The day that I die and the day that I am raised to life', 19:34. The passage in 3:48, 'I am about to cause thee to die and lift thee up to Me', is not clear. It need not necessarily mean more than it does in 6:60, where Allāh takes the souls of the sleepers to himself during their sleep and returns them when they awake years afterwards. However, in Arabic the verb normally means to die; but it is seldom safe to insist on interpreting the Qurān by later usage, as naturally it sometimes gave meanings to words which derive from the sense in which the Arabs understood them rather than from the true philological meaning. (A notable example of this is *ummī*, which unquestionably means 'gentile', but is everywhere taken to mean 'illiterate' because of the assumption that Muhammad could not write.)

He ascended into heaven. See what has just been said.

From thence He shall come. It is impossible to say what the Qurānic doctrine is here. The passage (4:156) which denies the crucifixion continues, 'and there are none of the people of the scriptures but will believe in him before his death and on the day of resurrection he will be a witness against them.' What does this mean? Does it mean that Jesus will return to the earth and Jews and Christians will believe in him as Muhammadan tradition asserts, or does it mean that confronted with Jesus in heaven on the day of judgement they will believe when it is too late and he will be a witness against those who rejected him? The question seems unanswerable. Another passage which might have thrown light on the subject is equally obscure: 43:61 reads, 'Verily he [Jesus] is a knowledge (*'ilm*) [or a sign (*'alam*) with another reading of the consonantal text giving it different vowels as some authorities do] of the Hour.' The first rendering makes very poor sense, and the second is difficult to interpret. At any rate it would seem to be impossible that Jesus could be a 'sign' of the Hour, i.e. of the end of all things, unless he were on earth. Some Muslim commentators take the Qurān to be the subject of the sentence. This would better fit the reading 'knowledge' and could possibly apply to 'sign'. No definite conclusion can be drawn from the Qurān. All that can be said is that there is a persistent tradition that Jesus will appear on earth again before the judgement day, and very early tradition asserted that he was to be seen on earth from time to time. Still, holding the view I do about *hadīth*, it would not be honest to appeal to it to prove something that is not clear in the Qurān.

Holy Ghost. See above.

Communion of Saints. The brotherhood of believers is a theme of the Qurān, but there is no suggestion of a doctrine of the communion of saints. This belongs to popular Islam. The tombs of holy men are visited, and prayers at their sepulchres are believed to be especially effective. But I know no straightforward text in support of such practices. The Wahhābīs have repressed such forms of piety with the utmost rigour.

Forgiveness of sins. This follows naturally from the doctrine of God in the Qurān.

Resurrection of the body. This was one of the central tenets of Muhammad's teaching.

The Life everlasting. Heaven and hell are described in vivid language in the Qurān. Heaven is a garden watered by rivers where grow rich fruits and flowers. There the Muslims drink the wine they have been denied on earth, wine that has no after-effects. It is brought to them by handsome youths, and dark-eyed houris wait on their every pleasure. Again and again the sensuous joys of Paradise are described in great detail. The faithful will be welcomed with the blessing of peace and see the angels round the throne of God, and join with them in declaiming the praise of God. Hell is a place of fire. It has seven gates, and a wall divides it from the heaven of the believers. The sufferings of the damned are described in horrific detail much as they were in medieval Europe.

From this rapid glance at the teaching of the Qurān as compared with Christianity it can be seen that the difference between them lies rather in what Islam denies than in what it affirms. It is agreed that God is the creator of the universe, that Jesus was miraculously born of a pure virgin, and that he ascended into heaven. It is agreed that there is a holy spirit; that God will forgive men's sins and grant them everlasting life if they obey his revealed will. With the negations we are not here concerned.

In conclusion, one cannot refrain from saying that the Muslim doctrine of God in philosophical theology is not so far removed from the Christian system until the crucial question of the Trinity comes into question. But even here the Ash'arites taught that God's attributes were additional to his essence and subsisted eternally in him, thus recognizing distinctions within the one Godhead. There are writers in Islam such as al-Ghazzālī whose deep spiritual insight command the respect of Christian readers, and there are mystics whose writings shine with the light of the illuminative life. The day may come when Muslims and Christians will realize that they have so much in common that they need no longer regard one another with suspicion and dislike. Such a rapprochement could only come about by an eclectic process.

Meanwhile all men of goodwill may take comfort from the words of the Secretary-General of the Arab League, Abdul-Rahman Azzam Pasha who, in a Christmas message a year or two ago, prayed that Christmas would remind the peoples of the world of the principles of peace and mercy that Christ taught. The Arabs, he said, would specially remember their Christian Arab brethren who stood shoulder to shoulder with them in the struggle in which they were engaged.

GLOSSARY

'*Abd.* Slave. Very common in names, e.g. 'Abdullāh.

Abū. Father of. Common in names, e.g. Abū Hāmid.

Ansār. Helpers. The first converts from Medina and finally the whole population who gave the prophet asylum and helped him in his campaigns.

Ashāb. Companions. In the widest sense everyone who saw and accompanied the prophet.

Darwīsh (dervish). Member of a religious fraternity.

Dhikr (*zikr*). Remembering; then mentioning. A technical term for the ritual recitations of the dervishes and their services.

Faqīr. One in physical or spiritual need. A mendicant dervish.

Fātiha. The opening chapter of the Qurān.

Fatwā. The formal opinion of a canon lawyer (*muftī*).

Hadīth. A technical term for a tradition of what the prophet said or did.

Hajj. The pilgrimage to Mecca.

Hijra (hegira). The prophet's flight to Medina from Mecca. The Muhammadan era dates from this year, A.D. 622.

Ibn. Son of. Corresponds to Hebrew *ben*.

Ijmā'. The consensus of the Islamic community. One of the foundations of law and practice.

Ijtihād. See *Mujtahid*.

Imām. Leader in the widest sense; then the leader of prayer in the mosque; the spiritual head of the Muslims.

Isnād. The chain of transmitters of a tradition.

Jihād. The duty to fight all unbelievers.

Jinn. Intelligent creatures of air and fire. In folklore and ancient poetry they resemble nymphs and satyrs and gods.

Ka'ba. The cube-like building in the centre of the mosque at Mecca.

Khalīfa (caliph). The lieutenant (of the prophet) and thus the head of all Muslims.

Masīhī. Christian, from Al-Masīh, the Christ.

Matn. The subject-matter of a tradition.

Mawālī. A term for freed slaves and then for non-Arab subjects generally. (For other meanings the Encyclopedia should be consulted.)

Midrash. A Hebrew word meaning 'study' and used technically of allegorical and pictorial expansions of biblical themes.

Miḥrāb. The niche at the east end of the mosque which gives the direction of Mecca.

Muftī. See *Fatwā*.

Muhājir. One who shared the *hijra* to Medina with the prophet.

Mujtahid. One who 'exerts himself' to form an opinion in legal matters. One who claims the right to reinterpret tradition.

Mutʿa. A temporary marriage for a stipulated time.

Nabī. Prophet.

Nasrānī. Nazarene, but the Qurān implies that the name should be connected with 'helper', not with Nazareth. In modern Arabics, a Christian.

Qāḍī (Cadi). Judge.

Qiyās. Analogy, especially in jurisprudence.

Rakʿa. Bending the body in prayer.

Rasūl. Someone sent. Apostle.

Ribāt. Monastery, generally fortified.

Sadaqa. Properly voluntary almsgiving as opposed to *zakāt*, the poor tax. The distinction was soon lost.

Saḥīḥ. Authentic, genuine.

Shāʿir. Poet. Originally a soothsayer or possessed person.

Shaykh. Old man, leader of a tribe, a title of respect. Especially used in connexion with the dervishes.

Shayṭān. Demon, akin to the jinn. The *Shayṭān* came to mean the chief of the evil spirits.

Shirk. The unforgivable sin of associating anyone or anything with Allāh.

Sunna (pl. *sunan*). Properly a custom or practice, and later narrowed down to the practice of the prophet or a tradition recording the same.

Taqīya. Shirking one's religious duty out of fear.

Zakāt. See *sadaqa*.

BOOKS FOR FURTHER READING

Only books written in English are mentioned, apart from a few standard
works in other European languages

CHAPTER ONE

W. R. SMITH: *The Religion of the Semites*. 3rd ed., London, 1927.
A classic.

D. S. MARGOLIOUTH: *The Relations between Arabs and Israelites
prior to the Rise of Islam* (Schweich Lectures). London, 1924.
For specialists.

FRANÇOIS NAU: *Les Arabes chrétiens de Mésopotamie et de Syrie du
VIIᵉ au VIIIᵉ siècle*. Paris, 1933.
The best work on the subject, based largely on Syriac writers.

J. WELLHAUSEN: *Reste arabischen Heidentums*. 2nd ed., Berlin,
1897.
A critical study, now somewhat antiquated.

The Encyclopedia of Islam.
This should be consulted on all points.

CHAPTER TWO

SIR WILLIAM MUIR: *The Life of Mohammad*. New ed., Edinburgh, 1923.
Keeps closely to the original sources, and though somewhat old-
fashioned is most useful.

FRANTS BUHL: *Das Leben Mohammeds*. Trans. H. H. Schaeder,
Berlin, 1930.
The best modern study.

TOR ANDRAE: *Mohammed, The Man and his Faith*. Eng. trans.,
London, 1936.
Brief and balanced.

ALFRED GUILLAUME: *The Life of Muhammad*, Oxford, 1955.
A translation of the standard biography of the prophet with introduction and notes.

ALFRED GUILLAUME: *New Light on the Life of Muhammad*,
Manchester, 1960.
Contains information not to be found elsewhere.

A full bibliography will be found in the *Encyclopedia of Islam*,
which has articles on all the subjects discussed in this book.

CHAPTER THREE

There are many English translations of the Qurān. George Sale's version (Chandos Classics) is still useful because it gives references to the standard Arabic commentaries. J. M. Rodwell's version (Everyman's Library) and E. H. Palmer's (World's Classics) are too literal to do justice to the original. M. Pickthall, *The Meaning of the Glorious Koran* (London, 1930), is often an interpretation rather than a translation. R. Bell (Edinburgh, 1937–9) is interesting. N. J. Dawood (Penguin Classics, 1956) is adequate. A. J. Arberry, *The Koran Interpreted* (London, 1955), is the best.

TH. NÖLDEKE: *Geschichte des Qorans.* 2nd ed., Leipzig, 1909–38.
> Indispensable to a critical study.

R. BELL: *The Origin of Islam in its Christian Environment.* London, 1926.
> Traces Christian influence from the Syrian churches.

H. U. W. STANTON: *The Teaching of the Qurān.* London, S.P.C.K., 1919.
> A useful summary.

J. JOMIER: *La Place du Coran dans la vie quotidienne en Égypte.* Tunis, 1952.
> Most informative.

R. F. BURTON: *A personal narrative of a pilgrimage to el-Medinah and Meccah.* London, 1855–6.

CHAPTER FOUR

C. BROCKELMANN: *History of the Islamic Peoples.* New York, 1947.
> Comprehensive and accurate.

P. K. HITTI: *History of the Arabs.* London, 1946.
> A critical study derived largely from Arabic sources.

B. LEWIS: *The Arabs in History.* London, Hutchinson's University Library, 1950.
> A masterly survey in small compass.

W. MUIR: *The Caliphate, its Rise, Decline, and Fall.* Edinburgh, 1924.
> Somewhat out of date, but still useful.

P. WITTEK: *The Rise of the Ottoman Empire.* London, 1938.
> Brief but valuable.

For regional histories see the literature cited in the *Encyclopedia of Islam*.

CHAPTER FIVE

J. SCHACHT: *The Origins of Muhammadan Jurisprudence*. Oxford, 1950.
   Invaluable.

I. GOLDZIHER: *Mohammedanische Studien*. Vol. ii, Halle 1890.
   Fundamental to the study of *hadīth*.

A. GUILLAUME: *The Traditions of Islam*. Oxford, 1924.
   Based partly on the last named.

M. MUHAMMAD ALI: *A Manual of Hadīth*. Lahore, n.d.
   A selection.

A. N. MATTHEWS: *A Translation of the Mishkat al-Masabih*. Calcutta, 1809.
   The only English translation of a selection of *hadīth* drawn from all the collections.

CHAPTER SIX

D. B. MACDONALD: *Development of Muslim Theology, Jurisprudence, and Constitutional Theory*. London, 1903.
   A good and clear account for its time; now rather outdated.

D. M. DONALDSON: *The Shī'ite Religion*. London, 1942.
   Descriptive and uncritical.

B. LEWIS: *The Origins of Ismā'īlism*. Cambridge, 1940.
   A critical study.

J. WINDROW SWEETMAN: *Islam and Christian Theology*. 2 vols., London, 1945–7 (further vols. to follow).
   A valuable study which throws much light on the doctrines of Muslim sects.

CHAPTER SEVEN

T. J. DE BOER: *The History of Philosophy in Islam*. London, 1933.
   A short sketch.

T. W. ARNOLD and A. GUILLAUME (editors): *The Legacy of Islam*. Oxford, 1931.

A. J. WENSINCK: *The Muslim Creed*. Cambridge, 1932.
   A scholarly analysis and discussion.

A. GUILLAUME: *Christian and Muslim Theology as represented by al-Shahrastani and St Thomas Aquinas.* (Bulletin of the School of Oriental and African Studies.) London, 1950.

CHAPTER EIGHT

R. A. NICHOLSON: *The Mystics of Islam.* London, 1914.

R. A. NICHOLSON: 'Mysticism' in *The Legacy of Israel* (ed. E. R. Bevan and C. Singer). Oxford, 1927.

A. J. ARBERRY: *Sufism.* London, 1950.

D. B. MACDONALD: *Aspects of Islam.* New York, 1911.

D. B. MACDONALD: *The Religious Attitude and Life in Islam.* Chicago, 1909.

J. P. BROWN: *The Darwishes or Oriental Spiritualism.* Ed. H. A. Rose. Oxford, 1927.

E. W. LANE: *The Manners and Customs of the Modern Egyptians.* London, Everyman's Library (first published in 1836).

CHAPTER NINE

C. C. ADAMS: *Islam and Modernism in Egypt.* London, 1933.

H. A. R. GIBB: *Whither Islam?* London, 1932.
 Deals with North Africa, India, Egypt, and Indonesia.

H. A. R. GIBB: *Modern Trends in Islam.* Chicago, 1947.

M. TITUS: *Indian Islam.* London, 1930.

MUHAMMAD IQBAL: *The Reconstruction of Religious Thought in Islam.* 2nd ed., London, 1934.

The Islamic Literature, various articles in 1952 and 1953.

J. N. D. ANDERSON: 'Recent Developments in Shari'a Law.' Nine articles in *The Moslem World,* Oct. 1950 to 1952.

J. N. D. ANDERSON: *The Problem of Divorce in the Shari'a Law of Islam.* Royal Central Asian Society, 1952.

J. N. D. ANDERSON: 'Recent Developments in Shari'a Law in the Sudan.' *Sudan Notes and Records,* 1950.

J. N. D. ANDERSON: 'The Personal Law of the Druse Community.' *The World of Islam,* 1950.

ASAF A. A. FYZEE: *Outlines of Muhammadan Law,* London, 1949.
 A full account of Muhammadan law in the Indian sub-continent.

INDEX

'Abbāssids, 82–4, 93, 114, 117, 166
Abraha, 13, 21
Abraham, 22, 44, 61, 63, 70, 109, 156
Abū Bakr, 32, 37, 39, 49, 57, 79, 96, 111
Abū Tālib, 24, 30, 34, 36
Abyssinia, 5, 13, 33, 62
Adam, 62, 118, 161
Africa, 85–6, 102, 113, 155
Ahmadīya, 125
'Ā'isha, 37, 81, 106, 172, 191
Algeria, 113, 181
'Alī, 27, 32, 39, 81–3, 112, 113, 115–118, 120, 121
Aligarh, university, 159
Amir 'Alī, Sayyid, 159
Anthropomorphism, 130, 135
Apostles, Muslim, 63, 88
Apostles' Creed, 194–8
Aristotle, 129, 136, 138–9
Ascension, 109, 136, 150
Asceticism, 144
Ash'arites, 140, 199
Ashraf, Shaykh Muhammad, 163 ff.
Assassins, 123–4
Averroes, 138–40

Badr, battle, 43, 44, 45
Baghdād, 84–6, 116, 128, 144, 147–8, 151
Bedouin, 2, 4, 13, 42, 45, 48
Berbers, 86, 113
Bible, Holy, 3, 8, 21, 58, 61, 85–6
al-Bukhārī, 91, 100
Byzantium, 5, 19, 33, 62, 78–80, 115, 117

Cairo, 75, 80, 85, 86
Camel, battle of the, 81
Christianity, 9, 13, 27, 160, 162, 194–9

Christians, 6, 12–13, 19, 33–4, 53, 62, 72, 86, 91, 118, 128
Companions, 90, 96, 99, 165, 170
Constantinople, 16, 18, 87, 115
Copts, 78
Creeds, Muslim, 134 ff.
Crusaders, 86, 123

Damascus, 13, 15, 19, 27, 79, 116, 144
Dante, 109, 150
Dervishes, 150, 152–4
Divorce, 71, 159, 163, 174, 183, 185
Druzes, 124–5

Egypt, 2–4, 11, 19, 66, 82, 84–5, 115, 155, 182, 185
conquest, 79, 80, 102
modernism in, 169–72, 175, 179, 182
Europe, 85, 87, 104, 161

Fasting, 69–70, 188
Fatalism, 161
Fātima, 27, 83, 112, 117, 120–1
Fiqh Akbar II, 118–19, 135

Gabriel, 34, 108–9, 189
al-Ghazzālī, 136, 138–40, 147–9, 161, 199
Greek Orthodox Church, 14, 78
philosophers, 128

al-Hakim bi-Amri'llāh, 124
Hallāj, 145–7, 149
Hanafī, 171, 174–5
al Hanafīya, 117
Hanbalites, 102
Heathens, 5, 6, 10, 27, 34, 61, 70, 114, 187
Heresy, 101, 111, 162
Hijāz, 4, 11–13, 16, 42, 94, 96, 99
Hijra, 3, 19, 23, 40
Hira, 9, 13, 15, 17, 79

Ibādis, 113
Ibn 'Arabī the Spaniard, 149–51
Ibn Ishāq, 21, 26, 32, 93–4, 99, 108, 190
Ibn Māja, 95, 100
Ibrāhīm ibn Adham, 144
Idolatry, 8, 40, 71, 119
Imām, 68, 103, 117–19, 120
India, 102, 121, 152, 163, 175
Indonesia, 102
Inheritance laws, 179–80, 184–8
Iqbāl, Sir Muhammad, 160
Iraq, 13, 24, 79, 83, 93–4, 99, 102, 115, 122, 169, 183
Ishmael, 3, 43, 61, 156
Ismā'īlīya, 84, 122–5

Ja'faris, 184–5
Jenghīz Khān, 86
Jerusalem, 12, 22, 43, 68, 79
Jesus, 14, 38, 43, 61, 109, 119, 121, 136, 145–6, 194–7
Jews, 10–13, 38, 40, 43, 47–8, 59, 60, 62, 81, 96, 118, 194, 197
Jihād, 42, 72
Jinn, 28, 37, 65
John of Ayla, 53
  the Baptist, 109
  St of Damascus, 93, 128
Jordan, 24, 169, 173, 182
Judaism, 9, 13, 27, 63, 68, 73, 130

Ka'ba, 10, 14, 31, 41, 43, 50, 61, 70, 151, 189
Kāzimayn, 105, 116
Khadīja, 5, 36
Khālid ibn al-Walīd, 50, 79
Khān, Sir Sayyid Ahmad, 159
Khārijites, 82, 111–14, 115, 144
Khazraj, 12, 24, 38, 39
Kūfa, 15, 58, 116

Law books, 93
  schools, 95, 102–3, 162, 169, 174
Lebanon, 123, 124, 169, 172

Mahdī, 117, 120, 121
Mālik ibn Anas, 89, 95, 99, 102, 122
Mamlūks, 86
Ma'mūn, 128
Marabouts, 152
Marriage, 103, 122, 172–3, 183–5, 186
Marwa, 50, 70
Mary, 14, 53
Mawālī, 80, 82, 116
Mecca, 4–6, 12, 16, 22–4, 39, 61, 67–68, 108–9, 117, 119, 123, 147, 156, 189
  conquest, 50–1
  pilgrimages to, 70
Medina, 4, 11, 12, 24, 31, 81, 95, 116
  Companions and Helpers, 111, 170
  law school, 102
  migration to, 39
  Muhammad's tomb, 70
  pilgrimage to, 102
  war with Mecca, 41
Minā, 38, 70
Missionaries, Muslim, 37–8
Mongols, 86, 121
Monophysites, 13, 14, 16, 17, 26, 34, 78
Monotheism, 8, 30, 38, 63
Morocco, 84, 122–3, 181
Mortmain, 180–2
Moses, 43, 109, 131, 135
Mosques, 68–9, 85, 105, 134
Mu'āwiya, 81–2, 112–13, 115–16
Muezzin, 66
Muftī, 102, 103, 170
Muhammad, 4–5, 8, 9, 12, 13, 16, 18, 23, 105, 118, 123, 189
  apostleship, 115
  birth, 23
  call, 24
  and Christianity, 38
  death, 53, 78–9
  epilepsy, 25–6

Muhammad—*contd*
 idea of, 149
 and idols, 119
 and laws, 99
 life of, 20–54
 marriage of, 27
 at Mecca, 14, 36, 50
 and monophysites, 26
 monotheism of, 30–1, 36
 poisoning, 49
 as prophet, 27–30
 sayings of, 89
 tolerance, 73
Muhammad Ali, 181
Murji'ites, 114–15
Muslim League, 124
Muslims, beginnings, 3, 6, 19, 33–4,
 40–1, 63
 in Europe, 85
Mu'tazila, 102, 113–14, 125, 129–34
Mysticism, 143–54

Nazarenes, 64
Nestorians, 14–15
Nu'mān, King, 15, 16, 18

Ottoman Empire, 86–7, 171, 181
Law of Family Rights, 172, 182,
 184

Pakistan, 124, 158, 164
Palestine, 2, 11, 12, 79
Persia, 17, 83, 84, 115, 121, 128
Persians, 4, 5, 15, 16, 18, 19, 78, 86,
 117, 122
Peruvians, 121
Philoponus, 139
Philosophers, 85
 Greek, 128
 Islamic, 135–8, 141
Pilgrimage, 70, 103
Pillars of Islam, 117
Plato, 129
Polygamy, 159–60

Prayer, at Ta'if, 36
 Muslim ritual, 66–8
Predestination, 132–5
Prophets, 28, 118, 119–20
Proverbs in Qurān, 76–7
Purdah, 160

Qadarites, 129
Qurān, 2, 4, 5, 7, 9, 12, 13, 20, 24, 25,
 31, 33, 42, 51, 55 ff., 62, 107, 113,
 119, 129, 134, 135, 145, 151, 153,
 155, 159, 164 ff.
 abrogations in, 186, 192
 alterations, 189
 in battle, 81
 and Bible, 58, 61, 194
 heaven and hell in, 161
 and human ego, 161
 on inheritance, 179–80, 186
 and Jesus, 14, 194–8
 as literature, 73–4
 on marriage, 103, 176
 missing verses, 191
 in mosques, 68
 Muhammad as author, 160
 and mysticism, 143
 and nature of God, 130
 recitation of, 75
 reconstruction, 51–60
 as sacred book, 72–4, 130–1
 Stoning, Verse of, 191
 and *sunna*, 95–7
 Sword, Verse of, 187
 teaching of, 63 ff.
 theologians on, 88
 Throne verse, 74, 75, 136, 143
 on women, 163, 166

Reformation of Islam, 158, 193
Resurrection, 9–10, 198
Romans, 4, 11, 12, 86

Sacrifices, 6, 70
Saints, 198

Saladin, 85
Sanūsī, 141
Saracens, 128
Satan, 62, 65, 189–90
Sauda, 37
Saʿūdī Arabia, 186
  dynasty, 114
Schisms, 79, 81
Seceders, 82
Selim, 87
Semites, 2, 78
Shāfiʿites, 102
Shariʿa, 97, 100, 101, 105, 118, 134, 157, 163, 171–2, 174, 185
Shayk of Islam, 103, 171
Shiʿa, 27, 31, 83, 114–25, 117, 119, 121, 170
Shiʿites, 101, 103–5, 183–5
Sicily, 18, 85, 86
Sin, 131
Slavery, 71, 160
Socrates, 136
Somaliland, 121
Spain, 84, 85, 138
Sudan, 121, 169, 174
Sūfis, 110, 143 ff., 161
Sumerians, 2, 59
Sunna, 88, 92, 94–6, 97, 100–1, 142, 147
Sunnis, 101, 103–5, 117–18, 119, 121–2, 129, 183–5

Syria, 2, 4, 5, 16, 17, 19, 53, 79, 81, 83, 85–6, 93–4, 112, 115–16, 122, 124, 128, 169, 173, 182

Ṭāʾif, 7, 36–7
Torah, 128
Trinity, 17, 199
Tunisia, 84
Turkestan, 193
Turkey, 152, 169, 181, 186
Turks, 18, 86, 87, 103, 166
Twelvers, 120–2

ʿUlamā, 100, 159, 160, 166, 182, 184, 192, 193
ʿUmar, 9, 34, 39, 44, 49–50, 54, 80, 81, 96, 97, 111, 113
ʿUmar Khayyām, 124
ʿUmmayad dynasty, 82–4, 89, 92, 94, 96, 98, 112–14
Unbelievers, 24
Universities, 85, 159
ʿUthmān, 57, 58, 81, 112, 191

Wahhābī, 102, 114, 198
Women in Islam, 71–2, 162, 192

Zanzibar, 113
Zayd, 57, 58, 191
Zaydis, 122
Zaynab, 27

MORE ABOUT PENGUINS
AND PELICANS

Penguinews, which appears every month, contains details of all the new books issued by Penguins as they are published. From time to time it is supplemented by *Penguins in Print*, which is a complete list of all books published by Penguins which are in print. (There are well over three thousand of these.)

A specimen copy of *Penguinews* will be sent to you free on request, and you can become a subscriber for the price of the postage. For a year's issues (including the complete lists) please send 30p if you live in the United Kingdom, or 60p if you live elsewhere. Just write to Dept EP, Penguin Books Ltd, Harmondsworth, Middlesex, enclosing a cheque or postal order, and your name will be added to the mailing list.

Some other books published by Penguins are described on the following pages.

Note: *Penguinews* and *Penguins in Print* are not available in the U.S.A. or Canada

THE STUDY OF RELIGIONS

H. D. Lewis and Robert Lawson Slater

'To maintain that all religions are paths leading to the same goal, as is so frequently done today, is to maintain something that is not true. Not only on the dogmatic, but on the mystical plane, too, there is no agreement.'

These downright words from an expert on oriental religion reflect the modern, realistic approach to the comparative study of religions. The results of western reappraisal of three great living traditions – Hinduism, Buddhism, and Islam – are outlined in the first part of this Pelican by Professor Slater, who discusses the history, literature, beliefs and practices of these religions and comments on their internal diversity and their attitudes to divinity. In the second part Professor H. D. Lewis relates trends in philosophy to the study of religions, examines the Hindu and Buddhist concepts of God, and questions whether such Christians as Paul Tillich have done well, in the high-minded cause of fraternity, to generalize their faith to the point at which it loses its essential Christianity. This book was originally published under the title *World Religions*.

BUDDHISM

Christmas Humphreys

The religion-philosophy known to the West as Buddhism is in number of adherents and range of teaching one of the largest in the world. Born in India in the sixth century B.C., it became the religion of Ceylon, Siam, Burma, and Cambodia, which adhere to the older or Southern School, while the developed Mahayana School is found in various forms in Tibet, Mongolia, China, Korea, and Japan. Its range of thought is equally vast. It includes the most exalted philosophy yet achieved by man, a psychology from which the West is slowly beginning to learn, a religion which has satisfied untold millions for 2,500 years, a Middle Way of self-development to self-enlightenment, and a range and depth of spiritual science, mysticism, and religious art which cannot be found elsewhere.

To compress such a wealth of human thought into a single volume is difficult, but here is not only the history and development of Buddhism and the teaching of the various Schools, but also its condition in the world today. On Buddhism in the West the author is an expert, having been President of the Buddhist Society, London, for thirty-three years; on world Buddhism he speaks with forty years' experience. The subject is now of special interest, in view of the vast changes that are taking place in Eastern Asia.

COMPARATIVE RELIGION

A. C. Bouquet

The story of the religious quest of mankind, its fruit, its failures, and its future prospects, is of supreme interest and great fascination, and much that is already known to specialists is not yet familiar to the general public. It is impossible to give full details in one short volume: but Dr Bouquet, who has specialized in the subject for over twenty years, here introduces readers to it, giving due attention to all parts of the world, and especially to India and the Far East.

He writes with scientific impartiality, and with full recognition of recent developments in the acquisition of knowledge: and he believes that there is only one right way of persuading, and that is to present what is true in such a way that nothing will prevent it from being seen except the desire to remain in darkness.

'His survey is well written, lucid and scholarly with pleasant touches of anecdotal humour to serve as leaven. It brings the subject up to date, and the author's grasp and treatment are admirable' – *Religions*.

'Altogether the book is a valuable book. It presents in small compass what Sir James Frazer did at considerably greater length, and it will be good for believers and unbelievers alike' – *Literary Guide*.

MYSTICISM IN
WORLD RELIGION

Sidney Spencer

This book by the Rev. Sidney Spencer is an explanation, for those who have found it hard to understand what mysticism is about, of the basic attitudes of mind which are common to mystics. In addition it describes, in terms which all can understand, the meaning of many key concepts such as 'self-annihilation', 'deification', 'the dark night of the soul', and of such movements as 'Gnosticism', 'The Heresy of the Free Spirit', and 'Sabbationism'.

The framework for this study is world religion, and the author describes and explains mystical thought in virtually all its contexts, primitive, Hindu, Chinese, Hellenistic, Hebrew, Christian and Moslem. The account is illustrated with numerous quotations from the sayings and writings of famous mystics. The final chapter surveys the main tendencies of mystical religion and their relevance to the recurring and fundamental problems of mankind.

HINDUISM

K. M. Sen

This book is a guide to the nature and function of Hinduism. Hinduism is unique among the great religions in that it had no founder but grew gradually over a period of five thousand years, absorbing and assimilating all the religions and cultural movements of India. Consequently it has no Bible or *Koran* or *Dhammapadam* to which controversies can be referred for resolution. Many works such as the *Vedas*, the *Upanishads* and the *Bhagavad-Gītā* are authoritative but none is exclusively so. As in Christianity there are several Hindu schools of thought, and *Hinduism* clearly outlines their common beliefs and particular differences.

A Penguin Classic

THE KORAN

Translated by N. J. Dawood

The Koran, as Mr Dawood claims, is not only one of the greatest books of prophetic literature but also a literary masterpiece of surpassing excellence. Unquestioningly accepted by Muslims to be the infallible word of Allah as revealed to Mohammed by the Angel Gabriel over thirteen hundred years ago, the Koran still provides the basic rules of conduct fundamental to the Arab way of life. Mr Dawood has produced a translation which retains the beauty of the original, altering the traditional arrangement to increase the understanding and pleasure for the uninitiated.

ANTHOLOGY OF ISLAMIC LITERATURE*

Edited by James Kritzeck

The literature of Islam is among the richest and the greatest in the world. Whether it has found expression in Arabic, Persian, Turkish, or any other of a dozen languages, this is a body of writing which preserves a distinct character of its own, largely because of a common religious influence. In the West, however, Islamic literature is hardly known at all, except by the specialist.

In this new anthology, now published for the first time in Britain, Professor Kritzeck has assembled the best available translations in verse and prose to represent the various periods of Islamic writing. The work he includes was all written before 1800.

These passages offer the general reader a unique introduction to a literature which, in the opinion of the experts, better exemplifies the Islamic genius than even the Alhambra or the Taj Mahal.

*NOT FOR SALE IN THE U.S.A. OR CANADA